WORLD CLUB

1

STUDENTS' BOOK

Michael Harris   David Mower

Longman

CONTENTS MAP

Module	Page	Vocabulary	Grammar	Skills
Planet Earth 5	47	actions; parts of the body; the weather	the present continuous – all forms	**Reading:** a tourist brochure **Listening:** a tourist guide; a quiz; a song **Speaking:** talk about our planet **Writing:** invent an alien
Villages 6	57	places and buildings; adjectives; jobs; free time activities	*there is / are*; *some* and *any*	**Reading:** tourist information; letters **Listening:** dialogues; a quiz about Britain **Speaking:** talk about your area; a shopping role-play **Writing:** invent a village
The Wild West 7	67	rooms; furniture; weapons; animals; verb	the past simple tense (regular verbs) – affirmative and negative	**Reading:** Native Americans; *The Little House*; Billy the Kid **Listening:** a story; a song **Speaking:** talk about life in the Wild West; talk about your own life **Writing:** a short biography
Travel 8	77	transport; countries; the weather; verbs; adjectives	the past simple tense – questions; irregular verbs	**Reading:** explorers; airships **Listening:** a story **Speaking:** tell a story **Writing:** an adventure story

Learning to learn

A Welcome

a

**Match the modules with the pictures.
Use the mini-dictionary on pages 98-105.**

Example: 1 b

1 Families
2 Cartoons
3 Hobbies
4 Parties
5 Planet Earth
6 Villages
7 The Wild West
8 Travel

b
QUIZ

• Find these items in the book.

Example: 1 page 42

1 A photo of a carnival.
2 Lesson 22: Gulliver's Travels.
3 Lesson 3: Animal Families.
4 A photo of a model ship.
5 A picture of Asterix.
6 A comic story.

c
Write a quiz like the one in exercise b.

d
In pairs, do your quiz.

Example: A: A picture of a shop.

B: Here, on page 62.

A: Yes, correct!

B Words

a KEYWORDS

Match the words with the pictures. Use the mini-dictionary on pages 98-105.

Example: pen 8

> pen bag rubber pencil dictionary
> students' book activity book ruler
> piece of paper notebook

b

In pairs, put some things in your bag. Guess your partner's things.

Example: A: A pen?
            B: No.

c

PRONUNCIATION

Listen to the alphabet and repeat the letters.

d KEYWORDS

Put the words in alphabetical order. Then test your partner's spelling.

Example: A: Spell 'alligator'.
            B: a-l-l-i-g-a-t-o-r.

> lion six alligator one eight kangaroo zebra
> dog five elephant cat three nine jaguar

e

Organise words in your vocabulary book alphabetically like this:

> K: kangaroo
>
> Kangaroos are from Australia.

Or by topics like this:

> animals
>
> lion tiger jaguar elephant kangaroo

C Classroom Language

a

Listen. Copy and complete.

please spell understand speak please you

1 I'm sorry, I don't ...

2 Can you ... more slowly, ...?

3 Can ... repeat that, ...?

4 Can you ... that, please?

Listen again and repeat.

b

In pairs, one person says words fast and the other writes them.

Example: A: A piece of paper.

B: I'm sorry, I don't understand. Can you speak more slowly, please?

A: A... piece... of... paper...

B: Can you spell *piece*, please?

A: P-i-e-c-e.

B: Thanks.

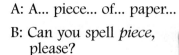

c

Listen and put the instructions in the order you hear them.

Example: 1 D

A
Listen to the story and answer the questions.

B
Read the story again. True or false?

C
Think of an animal. In pairs, ask questions about your partner's animal. Guess what it is.

D Language Focus
Copy and complete the table.

E
Look at the photo and write sentences about the people.

F KEYWORDS
Match the words in the box with the photos.

d

In pairs, give your partner a vocabulary test.

Example: A: What's ... in our language?

B: —.

A: Yes, right.

B: What's ... in English?

A: I don't know. Tiger?

B: No, wrong!

Families

Lead-in

Gómez

Fester

Grandma

Wednesday

Morticia

Pugsley

a 🔑 KEYWORDS

Look at the Addams Family. Match the words in the box with the names. Use the mini-dictionary on pages 98-105.

mother/son husband/wife father/daughter
brother/sister grandmother/grandson
uncle/nephew uncle/niece

Example: 1 husband/wife

1 Gómez/Morticia
2 Pugsley/Wednesday
3 Gómez/Wednesday
4 Grandma/Pugsley
5 Fester/Wednesday
6 Morticia/Pugsley
7 Fester/Pugsley

b

Imagine you are Pugsley or Wednesday. Test your partner.

Example: A: Fester and me.
B: Uncle and niece.
A: Yes, right.

1 A Nepalese Family

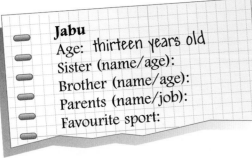

A village family

A

Look at the pictures and read the text. Who are the people?

Example: 1 Norbu

B

Read the text again. Copy and complete the information.

Jabu
Age: thirteen years old
Sister (name/age):
Brother (name/age):
Parents (name/job):
Favourite sport:

Jabu and his family are from a village in the Himalayas in Nepal. Jabu is thirteen years old. His sister is called Pomzi and she's four years old. His brother Norbu is two years old. His father is called Kepu and his mother Cheuki. His grandmother is called Bajai and she lives with the family.

His parents are farmers in the village and they aren't rich. Their house is small and it isn't very modern, but it's warm in the winter. Jabu is a pupil in the village school and he helps his mother and father on the farm. His favourite sport is badminton and he plays it with his friends in the village. They're very good players!

Language Focus: *To be*

C

Copy and complete the tables.

Example: 1 are

AFFIRMATIVE		
I	am ('m)	
you / we / they	¹ ... ('re)	from Nepal.
he / she / it	² ... ('s)	

NEGATIVE		
I	am not ('m not)	
you / we / they	³ ... (aren't)	rich.
he / she / it	is not (⁴ ...)	

D

Copy and complete the sentences about Jabu.

Example: 1 am

1   I ... thirteen years old.
2   We ... from Nepal.
3   My family ... from a village.
4   My parents ... farmers.
5   My house ... very modern.
6   My favourite sport ... football.
7   I ... from Britain.
8   My parents ... teachers.
9   My house ... very warm in winter.
10 We ... from Spain.

E

WHO IS IT?

• Complete this personal information on a piece of paper.

> I'm from ...
> My parents are called ...
> My birthday is in ... (month)
> My favourite sport is ...
> My favourite film is ...

• In groups, mix up the pieces of paper. One student reads the sentences and the others guess who it is.

F  DICTIONARY SKILLS

Put these words in alphabetical order. Then check your answers in the mini-dictionary.

1   warm   modern   village   winter   friend   favourite
2   pen   pencil   paper   partner   parents   pupil
3   school   sport   swim   spell   small   sentence

(EXTRA TIME)

Look at World Club magazine on page 88. Do activity 1.

2 Twins

A KEYWORDS

Which words in the box are similar in your language? Use the mini-dictionary.

> identical similar different
> sporty fantastic sociable quiet
> favourite good small strange

B

Read about these identical twins. Copy and complete the family tree.

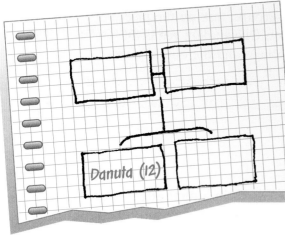

Danuta (12)

C

Read the text again. Copy and complete the table.

	Danuta	Magda
Personality	sociable	quiet
Age		
Favourite group/singer		
Favourite sport		
Favourite subjects		

Dear Alice,

My name is Danuta and I'm twelve years old. I am from San Diego in California. Magda is with me in the photo – she is my twin sister. I'm on the right! It's very strange – Magda and I are identical twins, but we're very different. We're both very sporty, but I'm very sociable and Magda is quiet.

Our favourite sport is basketball and we are in the school team. My favourite group is The Prodigy – they're fantastic! Magda likes Janet Jackson. My favourite subjects at school are geography and science. Magda prefers English and history.

Our parents are from Poland. My dad is called Stan. He's forty-two. My mum is called Ewa and she's thirty-nine. She's a doctor at a hospital in San Diego.

Write to me soon.

Love,

Danuta

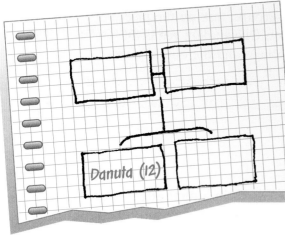

Families

D

List words from the text.

1 you can guess – they are similar in your language.

2 you can't guess – use the mini-dictionary.

E

Join these sentences with *and*.

Example: 1 My favourite sport is football and I'm a good player.

1 My favourite sport is football. I'm a good player.

2 I am sociable. I am sporty.

3 My dad is called David. He's from Alicante.

4 My mum is called Rosa. She's from Lugo.

5 She is quiet. She is strange.

F

Punctuate the letter using capital letters and full stops.

Example: Dear Carlos,

Hi! My name's Daniel...

Dear carlos,
hi! my name's daniel i'm thirteen years old and i'm from london i'm very sporty my favourite sport is tennis and i'm a good player my favourite group is pearl jam my favourite school subject is art i'm not a very good pupil!
write to me soon
Daniel

G

Re-write the letter in exercise F about yourself. Include one false piece of information.

Sports: basketball tennis football cycling swimming

School subjects: maths English history science geography

H

In pairs, read your letters and guess the false information.

Example: A: Your favourite subject isn't maths!

B: No, it isn't. My favourite subject is art.

Did you know?

Every year, thousands of twins have a party in Twinsburg, Ohio, in the U.S.A – a town started by twins.

EXTRA TIME

Look at World Club magazine on page 88. Do activity 2.

3 Animal Families

A KEYWORDS

What colours are the animals?

Example: Elephants are grey.

blue orange yellow grey green red black white brown pink purple

B KEYWORDS

Which animals are *mammals*? Which are *birds*? Which are *cats*?

Example: Polar bears are mammals.

C ANIMAL QUIZ

• Listen and guess the animals from exercise A.

Example: 1 tiger

Language Focus: Questions

D

Look at the word order in these examples:

YES/NO QUESTIONS		
Is	it	a tiger?
Are	they	from Africa?

ANSWERS
Yes, it is.
No, they aren't.

WH- QUESTIONS		
Where	is	it from?
What	are	your favourite animals?

ANSWERS
Asia.
Cats.

Listen to part 1 of the quiz again and match these questions and answers.

1 Where is it from?
2 Is it big?
3 What colour is it?
4 Is it a lion?

a No, it isn't.
b Yes, it is.
c Asia.
d Yellow and black.

E

Match these questions and answers.

Example: 1 b

1	What are your favourite animals?	**a** No, they aren't.
2	Are you sporty?	**b** Elephants and dolphins.
3	How old are you?	**c** Blur.
4	Who is your favourite group?	**d** No, I'm not.
5	Are penguins from the Arctic?	**e** Antarctica.
6	Where are they from?	**f** I'm twelve.

F

Write questions for these answers.

Example: 1 Where are you from?

1 I'm from Caceres. (Where ...)
2 No, he isn't from Vigo. (Is ...)
3 Yes, kangaroos are from Australia. (Are ...)
4 My teacher is Mrs Evans. (Who ...)
5 Elena is thirteen. (How old ...)
6 Yes, I'm a good student. (Are ...)
7 It's grey. (What colour ...)

G

PRONUNCIATION: QUESTIONS

Listen and check your questions from exercise F. Then repeat the questions.

H

GUESS THE ANIMAL

• Think of an animal. In pairs, ask questions about your partner's animal. Guess what it is.

Example:

A: Is it a bird?   B: Yes, it is.
A: What colour is it? B: Black and white.
A: Where is it from? B: Antarctica.
A: Is it a penguin?   B: Yes, it is.

Did you know?

There are more than 9,000 different types of birds.

Look at World Club magazine on page 88. Do activity 3.

Fluency

Writing: A Description

A

In groups, invent and describe a strange family.

Stage 1: Preparation

In groups, decide who is in the family. Write notes about the people in a table.

Example:

Name	Dr 'X-ray' Strange	Abnorma Strange	'Tiger' Strange	The twins: April + June
Age	43	31	12	2
Job	a doctor	basketball player	school pupil	
Favourite colours	black and white	purple and pink	black and orange	black and white
Hobby	collecting skeletons	playing chess	collecting spiders	swimming

Stage 2: Writing

Use your table to write a description. Each student in the group writes about one person in the family. Remember to use capital letters and full stops.

> The Strange family.
> Dr X-ray Strange is a doctor and he is forty-three. His hobby is collecting skeletons and his favourite colours are black and white.

Stage 3: Checking

Check your descriptions. Look at the Keyword Check and Grammar References 1 and 2 on page 16.

Stage 4: Display

Copy your descriptions neatly and draw pictures of the people. Show your friends or display them on the wall.

Speaking: Finding Out Information

B

In pairs with a student from a different group, ask questions about the families.

Where are they from?
Who is in the family?

What is his/her job?
How old is he/she?

What is his/her favourite colour?
What is his/her hobby?

Listening: A Quiz

C

Listen and answer the questions – choose a, b or c. Then check the answers with your teacher.

Consolidation

Grammar

A

Correct these sentences.

Example: 1 My father is thirty-five (or thirty-five years old).

1 My father is *thirty-five years.*
2 Where *he is* from?
3 *He from* Gdansk.
4 My mother *is engineer.*
5 I'm *no sporty.*

B

Complete the text with these words:

isn't (x2) / is (x5) / are (x2) / aren't

Example: 1 are

In our family, animals ¹... very important. Bouncer ²... a brown and white Cocker Spaniel. He ³... very active – his hobby is sleeping! Patch ⁴... a cat and he ⁵... twelve years old. Kate, Naomi and Claudia ⁶... goldfish. They ⁷... very sociable! Harry ⁸... my parrot. His favourite expression ⁹..., 'Can you repeat that, please? Can you repeat that, please? Can you repeat that, please?' – he ¹⁰... my favourite animal!

C

Order these words to make questions.

Example: 1 Are you from Turkey?

1 from / you / Turkey / are?
2 favourite / what / music / your / is?
3 how / old / he / is?
4 your / what / is / name?
5 Africa / parrots / are / from?

Vocabulary

D

Copy and complete the table with words from the box. Write new words in your vocabulary book.

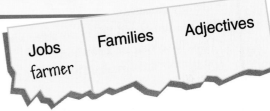

husband farmer teacher rich quiet wife nephew doctor strange uncle engineer sociable

Jobs — farmer

Families

Adjectives

Pronunciation: Contractions

E

Listen and count the words. Short forms count as two words.

Example: I'm not very sporty. 5 words

1 2 3 4 5

Listen again and repeat the sentences.

F

ALPHABET BINGO

- Copy this square but write different letters.
- Listen to the letters on the cassette. Cover your letters when you hear them. If you cover nine squares, shout 'Bingo' - you are the winner!

F	G	A
I	E	B
C	L	O

Module check

Grammar Reference

1 To be

	Affirmative	Negative
I	am	am not ('m not)
you/we/they	are	are not (aren't)
he/she/it	is	is not (isn't)

To be is a **main verb** or an **auxiliary**.

As a **main verb** it is used to:

• Identify ourselves:

Hi! I'm Danuta and this is my sister Magda.

• Describe a state or a condition:

The parents are farmers. They aren't rich.

• Indicate a position:

Magda is with me in the photo. I'm on the right.

• Say where we come from:

My dad is from Rosario.

• Express age:

Jabu is thirteen years old.

2 Yes/no and *wh-* questions: *to be*

Questions			
Who	am	I?	
What	are	you/we/they?	
Where	is	he/she/it?	
	Am	I	
	Are	you/we/they	British?
	Is	he/she/it	

• Wh- questions begin with **who / what / where / how**, etc.

• Yes/no questions begin with the verb *to be*.

• You can answer *yes/no* questions with *yes* or *no* or with a *short answer*:

Are penguins from Antarctica? Yes. / Yes, they are.

Is Jabu from Africa? No. / No, he **isn't**.

Keyword Check KEYWORDS

Families: aunt, brother, daughter, father, granddaughter, grandfather, grandmother, grandson, mother, nephew, niece, parents, sister, son, uncle

Adjectives: bad, big, cold, different, fantastic, favourite, good, identical, modern, quiet, rich, similar, small, sociable, sporty

Sports: basketball, badminton, cycling, football, swimming, tennis

School subjects: art, English, geography, history, maths, science

People: doctor, engineer, farmer, teacher

Animals: elephant, kangaroo, lion, parrot, penguin, tiger, polar bear, mammal

Colours: black, blue, brown, green, grey, orange, pink, purple, red, white, yellow

Classroom language:

Look at the photo.

Match the words and the names.

Draw your family tree.

Copy and complete the table.

Use the mini-dictionary.

Check your description.

Correct these mistakes.

1 **Look at Grammar References 1-2 above and complete Grammar Files 1-2 in the Activity Book. Then do the *Test Yourself: Grammar* on page 11 of the Activity Book.**

2 **Look at the Keyword Check. Write important new words in your vocabulary book. Then do the *Test Yourself: Vocabulary* on page 11 of the Activity Book.**

Cartoons

Lead-in

Module 2

2

MODULE OBJECTIVES

IN THIS MODULE YOU WILL …

Read a comic story and an interview.
Listen to descriptions and music.
Talk about cartoon characters.
Practise using *can* and *has got*.
Draw a cartoon character and write a description.

a ✍

List your five favourite cartoons.

Example: The Pink Panther, The Simpsons

b 🗣 📖 KEYWORDS

**In groups, read your list and give opinions.
Use these words. Add up the points.**

great / very funny - 5 points
OK / sometimes funny - 3 points
boring / terrible - 0 points

Example: A: Spiderman.
B: I think he's great. (5 points)
C: I think he's boring. (0 points)
D: I think he's OK. (3 points)

c 🗣

Tell the class about your group's favourite cartoons.

Example: Our favourite cartoons are Popeye and Scooby Doo.

4 Supertwins!

A

Read the story. True or false?

1 On the first day, Mike can do the maths exercise.
2 Mandy can play volleyball well.
3 The alien gives them magic pens.
4 The next day Mike can do his maths exercises.
5 The next day Mandy can play basketball very well.

Language Focus: *Can*

B

Look at examples of *can* in the story. Copy and complete the tables.

AFFIRMATIVE		
I / you / he / she / it / we / they	¹...	fly.

NEGATIVE		
I / you / he / she / it / we / they	²...	fly.

QUESTION		
³...	I / you / he / she / it / we / they	fly?

SHORT ANSWER		
Yes,	I / you / he / she / it / we / they	⁴...
No,		can't.

C

Look at the activities in the box. Write sentences about what you *can* or *can't* do.

Example: I can ride a bicycle.

> ride a bicycle   play chess   draw cartoons
> cook a hamburger   sing a song in English
> swim underwater   swim 200 metres   jump two metres
> say the alphabet in English   count to 100 in English

D

In pairs, ask your partner questions from exercise C. Give short answers.

Example: A: Can you play chess?
　　　　　B: No, I can't.

E

SPELLING GAME

> • Write down five words from modules 1 and 2.
> • In pairs, test your partner.
> *Example:* A: Can you spell daughter?
> 　　　　　B: Yes, I can. D-A-U-G-H-T-E-R.
> 　　　　　A: Correct!

Did you know?
Batman can't fly.

(EXTRA TIME)

Look at World Club magazine on page 89.
Do activity 4.

5 Drawing

A KEYWORDS

Match the words in the box with the numbers on the drawings above.

long hair   short hair   pointed ears
hat small nose   big mouth   eyebrows
earrings   moustache   big eyes

B

Match the sentences with the drawings. Listen to the cartoonist and put the drawings in order.

1 Add the nose and mouth.
2 Draw a head and divide it into four.
3 Add things ~ a hat, earrings or moustache.
4 Draw the eyes and ears.
5 Draw the hair and eyebrows.

C

Listen to a description of a cartoon character. Draw the character as you listen. Show the drawing to your partner.

D

PRONUNCIATION: CAN/CAN'T
Listen and repeat the sentences.

E

Imagine things about the girl in your drawing. Complete these sentences about her.

1 ... is from ...
2 *She* can play ...
3 *She* can't ... very well.
4 *Her* brother is called ...
5 *He* can ...
6 *He* can't ...

F

In pairs, ask and answer questions about the girl.

Example: A: What's her name?
B: Florence.
A: What can she do?

G
DICTIONARY SKILLS

Are these words correctly spelt? Use the mini-dictionary.

1 favourete   4 geograpy
2 alphabet   5 diferent
3 bicicle   6 similar

Look at World Club magazine on page 89. Do activity 5.

6 The Silly Family

Gertrude

Grandpa

Horace

Grandma

Darlene

Rudolf

LIMO 1

A  KEYWORDS

Look at the picture. Choose the correct words.

1 Grandpa is *tall / short*.
2 Grandma is *fat / thin*.
3 Rudolf has got a *big / small* nose.
4 Horace has got *long / short* hair.
5 Gertrude has got *dark / fair* hair.
6 Rudolf and Gertrude have got *brown / green* eyes.

B

Read the interview with Rudolph. Find *five* differences between the text and the picture. Copy and complete the table.

In the picture ...	In the text ...
five piranha fish	ten piranha fish

Have you got any pets, Rudolf?

Yes, we have.

What animals have you got?

We've got a tarantula called Maggie, an alligator called Alistair and ten piranha fish.

Tell us about your house.

It's very silly, of course. It hasn't got a big garden. But our car is very big – it has got a TV in it!

Tell us about your family.

My mum is called Gertrude. She's 37. She is tall and she has got blonde hair. Her eyes are green and she's got a small nose. My dad is called Horace and he's 40. He is short and he has got blue eyes. He's got very long, dark hair.

What about you?

My name is Rudolph Silly and I'm eleven. I've got black hair and green eyes.

And your sister?

Darlene is six. She is short and fat with fair hair and brown eyes. She's got a very big nose!

Tell us about your grandparents.

They are very old. They haven't got pets or a car, but they've got lots of interesting books. Grandpa is tall and he's got short, white hair. Grandma has got black hair.

Thank you, Rudolph.

Language Focus: *Has got/have got*

C

Look at the text. Copy and complete the boxes.

AFFIRMATIVE

I	have ('ve)		black hair.
he			blue eyes.
she	[1]... ([2]...)		blond hair.
it		got	a TV in it.
we			a tarantula.
they	[3]... ([4]...)		lots of books.

NEGATIVE

It	has not ([5]...)	got	a garden.
They	[6]... (haven't)		pets.

QUESTIONS

	[7]...	you	got	any pets?
What	[8]...	you	got?	

SHORT ANSWERS

Yes, he has.	No, he hasn't.
Yes, we [9]...	No, we haven't.

D

Complete with *have/has* (+) or *haven't/hasn't* (-).

Example: We *have* got a small house.

1 We ... got a small house. (+)
2 It ... got a big garden. (–)
3 We ... got any pets. (–)
4 I ... got a Walkman (+), but I ... got a lot of cassettes. (–)
5 My big brother ... got a computer. (+)
6 My parents ... got two cars. (+)

E

Complete these questions.

Example: Have you got a computer?

1 you / got a computer?
2 your house / got a garden?
3 you / got any pets?
4 your mother / got long hair?
5 you / got a lot of books?
6 your family / got a car?

F

In pairs, ask your partner the questions.

G

MEMORY GAME

• Write four questions about the Silly family. Cover the picture and the text. In pairs, ask and answer the question.

Example: A: Have they got a dog?
B: No, they haven't.

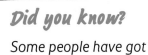

EXTRA TIME

Look at World Club magazine on page 90.
Do activity 6.

Fluency

Writing: My Cartoon Character

A

Draw your own cartoon character and write a description.

Stage 1: Preparation

Draw a simple cartoon character. Do not show it to your friends. Make notes about it.

Example:

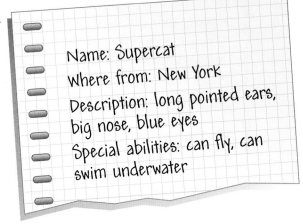

Name: Supercat
Where from: New York
Description: long pointed ears, big nose, blue eyes
Special abilities: can fly, can swim underwater

Stage 2: Writing

Write a description of your character.
Use adjectives, *has got* and *can*.

Stage 3: Checking

Check your descriptions for mistakes. Look at the Grammar Reference on page 26.

Speaking: Describe and Draw

B

Describe your cartoon character to your partner. He/she draws it.

Stage 1: Preparation

Practise saying your description. The words in the box will help you.

Example: My character is a cat. He has got long, pointed ears.

> head eyes ears nose earrings
> glasses mouth hair eyebrows hat
> moustache face
> big/small green/blue/brown tall/short
> pointed/round/square fat/thin

Stage 2: Speaking

Do *not* show your drawing to your partner.

Describe your character. Your partner draws it.

Compare the two drawings.

Listening: Cartoon Quiz

C

Listen and answer the questions a, b or c.

Example: 1 c

Consolidation

Grammar

A

Write questions with *can* and then answer them using short answers.

Example: 1 Can penguins fly? No, they can't.

1 penguins / fly?
2 you / sing?
3 your mother / speak English?
4 your father / play chess?
5 you / speak French?
6 Batman / fly?

B

Complete the sentences with *have/has* (+), *haven't/hasn't* (-).

1 We ... got two dogs, a cat and three fish. (+)
2 My mother can't drive. She ... got a car. (–)
3 Sophie ... got a lot of cartoons on video. (+)
4 They ... got a big house. It ... got a small garden. (–)
5 Martin ... got a computer. (+)

C

Write questions with *has got* or *have got*. Then write short answers.

Example: 1 Has your school got a computer room?   Yes, it has.

1 your school / a computer room?
2 the Flintstones / a pet?
3 Bill Gates / a lot of money?
4 Superman / fair hair?
5 Claudia Schiffer / long hair?
6 the Sillies / a dog?

D

MEMORY GAME

• In groups, play this memory game. If you make a mistake, you are out.

Ana: I've got a dog called Jo.
Magda: Ana has got a dog called Jo and I've got a poster of Leonardo DiCaprio.
Juan: Ana has got a dog called Jo, Magda has got a poster of Leonardo DiCaprio, and I've got a computer.

Vocabulary

E

Match the verbs and nouns.

Example: speak English

speak play do ride draw sing read cook

a hamburger mathematics a bicycle
books cartoons songs basketball English

Pronunciation: Contractions

F

Listen and count the words in each sentence. Contractions count as two words. Then listen again and write down the sentences.

Example: She's from London. = 4 words
          1 2 3   4

Module check

Grammar Reference

3 Can

I/you/he/she/it/we/they	Affirmative	Negative
	can play	can't play (can not)

Questions			
What When Where	can	I/you/he/she/it/ we/they	read?
	Can		

- Can is used to express ability:

He can ride a bicycle. I can't play chess.

- Remember! You can answer can questions with *yes, no* or a *short answer*:

Can you spell 'daughter'? Yes. / Yes, I can.

Can you speak Japanese? No. / No, we can't.

4 Has / have got

	Affirmative	Negative	Questions			
I/you/ we/ they	have got	have not got (haven't got)	Have	I/you/ we/they	got	a car?
he/ she/it	has got	has not got (hasn't got)	Has	he/she/it	got	a car?

- Has/have got is used to indicate possession:

He's got ten piranha fish. They've got lots of books. I've got black hair and green eyes.

- Remember! You can answer has/have got questions with *yes* or *no* or with a *short answer*:

Has he got an alligator? Yes. / Yes, he has.

Have you got a big nose? No! / No, I haven't.

Keyword Check 🔑 KEYWORDS

Opinions: I think it's boring / excellent / funny / good / great / interesting / OK / terrible / useless

Activities: cook (hamburgers), count (to 100), do (mathematics), draw (pictures / cartoons), fly, jump (two metres), play (sport), say (the alphabet), sing (songs), speak (French), swim (underwater)

Parts of the body: face, head, hair, ears, nose, mouth, eyebrows, moustache, eyes

Descriptions: big/small, fair/dark, fat/thin, round/square, short/tall, tall/short

Possessions: bicycle, car, cassette, computer, earrings, garden, glasses, hat, house, pet, poster, Walkman

Animals: alligator, piranha fish, tarantula

Classroom language:
Tell the class.
Take turns to ...
Put the pictures in order.
Choose the correct words.
Make notes about ...
Complete the sentences with ...
Check your writing.

1 Look at Grammar References 3-4 above and complete Grammar Files 3-4 in the Activity Book. Then do the *Test Yourself: Grammar* on page 18 of the Activity Book.

2 Look at the Keyword Check. Write important new words in your vocabulary book. Then do *Test Yourself: Vocabulary* on page 18 of the Activity Book.

Hobbies
Lead-in

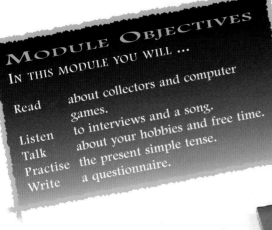

MODULE OBJECTIVES
IN THIS MODULE YOU WILL …

Read   about collectors and computer games.
Listen   to interviews and a song.
Talk   about your hobbies and free time.
Practise the present simple tense.
Write   a questionnaire.

a  KEYWORDS

**Look at the picture and the words in the box.
List your hobbies.**

Example: football

play: basketball, football, computer games, tennis, table tennis, chess

collect: keyrings, stickers, stamps, coins, badges

make: model planes, model cars

read: comics, books, magazines

play: the violin, the piano, the guitar

b

In groups, read your list. What are the favourite hobbies in each group?

Example: football (3 people)
           comics (2 people)

7 Collecting

A

What do you collect? Tell the class.

Example: I collect badges. I've got about 50.

B

Look at the photos. Guess the answers to these questions. Read and check.

1 Miriam collects
   a) badges b) national dolls c) coins

2 She has got
   a) fifteen b) twenty c) twenty-five

3 Her favourite doll is
   a) Japanese b) Spanish c) Russian

4 Simon makes and collects
   a) model cars b) model ships c) model aeroplanes

5 He has got
   a) fifteen b) twenty-five c) thirty

6 His favourite ships are
   a) old   b) very big c) modern

LETTERS PAGE

This week - collecting things

I collect national dolls. I have got about twenty dolls from different countries like Greece, Holland and Japan. My favourite doll is from Japan. My parents give me dolls on my birthday. I also buy dolls when we go on holiday. I keep the dolls in my bedroom – I don't want my little brother to play with them!
Miriam Davies, Swansea

I make and collect model ships. I have got about thirty models of old boats (I don't collect modern ships). I make them from kits and paint them. I've also got three radio-controlled ships — my dad helps me make them. My favourite boat is a tall ship — it's fantastic! On Sundays we sail the ships in the park. My dad doesn't sail the tall ship because it's expensive and he doesn't want to crash it!

Simon Bartlett, Belfast

Language Focus: Present Simple

C

Copy and complete the tables. Look at examples in the text.

AFFIRMATIVE		
I / you / we / they	[1]...	national dolls.
he / she / it	collects	

NEGATIVE		
I / You / We / They	don't want	to crash it.
He / She / It	[2]...	

D

Complete these sentences with the correct form of the verb.

Example: 1 gives

My mum [1] ... *(give)* me dolls on my birthday. She [2] ... *(go)* to lots of different places for her work. My friends [3] ... *(not play)* with dolls. They [4] ... *(collect)* pop posters. My brother [5] ... *(not go)* in my room.

I [6] ... *(make)* model aeroplanes. I [7] ... *(not play)* with them - they are not toys. My dad [8] ... *(buy)* me kits. He [9] ... *(help)* me to make them, but he [10] ... *(not fly)* them.

E

Write sentences about hobbies.

Example: We don't watch TV.

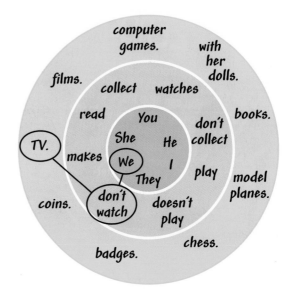

F

In pairs, say true and false sentences about your friends. Your partner guesses the false sentences.

Example: A: Alicia collects dolls.
 B: True.
 A: No, false!

G
 DICTIONARY SKILLS

Are these words nouns, verbs or adjectives? Look them up in the mini-dictionary.

1 badge
2 make
3 song
4 interesting
5 speak
6 thin

 EXTRA TIME

Look at World Club magazine on page 90. Do activity 7.

Hobbies

8 Game Power

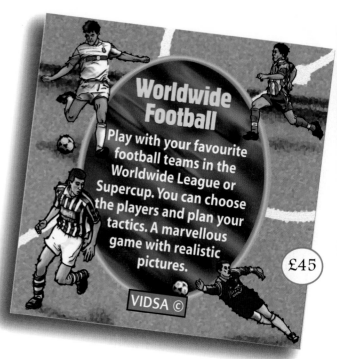

£32

£45

CPR Games

VIDSA ©

Hobbies

A  KEYWORDS

Choose your three favourite games.

card games chess dominoes ludo
Game Boy Monopoly Scrabble
interactive computer games
Trivial Pursuit word puzzles

B

In pairs, talk about your favourite games.

Example:

A: My favourite game is a computer game called Haunted House. It's brilliant.

B: My favourite is Trivial Pursuit. I love quiz games.

A: I also like ...

C

Look at the computer game covers quickly. Match them with these topics:

• sport   • war   • clothes

D

Read about the games and choose your favourite. Copy the table and make notes.

	Planet Zenda	Worldwide Football	Fashion Show
Interesting	no	yes	yes
Original			
Creative			
Expensive			

Fashion Show

You are an international fashion designer. You make clothes for top models. Choose materials, colours and designs. This game gives you realistic images of supermodels like Claudia Schiffer and Cindy Crawford - with your clothes! Give your friends a private fashion show!

BFG©

£65

F

Write a letter to *World Club Magazine* about the games you play. Use the words in the box to help you and include the word *also*.

Where? at home / at school / at my friend's house

When? at weekends / in the evenings / after school / on holiday

Who with? with my friends / with my family / on my own

Example:

I love Game Boy. I play at home after school. I play on my own and also with my friends. I also like computer games. I play with my sister in the evenings. Our favourite games are Bermuda Triangle and Art Mania.

Natalia Gómez, Río Gallegos

E  KEYWORDS

Match the adjectives with the definitions.

1 exciting
2 sinister
3 marvellous
4 private

a strange and nasty
b very interesting
c personal
d very good

Did you know?

The game of dominoes is originally from China, and chess is from Iran.

EXTRA TIME

Look at World Club magazine on page 91. Do activity 8.

9 Outdoors

A  KEYWORDS

Match the drawings below with the words in the box.

swimming   sailing   canoeing
cycling   horse riding   surfing   skiing
tennis   football   beach volleyball

B 🎞

Look at the photos and questions and guess the answers for Silvia and Paul.

Example: 1 Silvia = a, Paul = c

1 When do they go canoeing/play football?
   a) summer b) winter c) all the year
2 Where do they do the sports?
   a) on the coast b) in the mountains
   c) in the city
3 Who do they do them with?
   a) with their friends b) with their family
   c) with a club

Listen to the interviews and check your answers.

Language Focus: Present Simple: *Yes/No* Questions

C

Look at the tables. What are the questions and answers in your language?

YES/NO QUESTIONS			
Do	I / you / we / they	**play**	football?
Does	he / she / it		

SHORT ANSWERS		
Yes,	I / you / we / they	**do.**
No,		**don't.**
Yes,	he / she / it	**does.**
No,		**doesn't.**

D

Use the words to write *yes/no* questions.

Example: 1 Do you play tennis?

1 you play tennis?
2 they go canoeing?
3 he play beach volleyball?
4 her brother go sailing?
5 you play in the evenings?
6 she go to a club?

E

In pairs, ask and answer questions.

| play football   go swimming   play tennis |
| go skiing   go cycling   play basketball |

Example: A: Do you play football?
          B: No, I don't.

Language Focus: Present Simple: *Wh-* Questions

F

Look at the table. Then write questions.

WH- QUESTIONS			
When Where	**do**	I / you / we / they	**play?**
What	**does**	he / she / it	

Example: 1 What sport do you play?

1 What sport / you play?
2 Where / you go skiing?
3 Who / he play football with?
4 When / she go canoeing?
5 Where / you play football?
6 Where / he go cycling?

Write five more *Wh-* questions about sports.

G

In pairs, ask and answer questions about your favourite activities.

Example: A: What do you do?
          B: I play tennis.
          A: Who do you play with?
          B: My friend, Sam.

(EXTRA TIME)

Look at World Club magazine on page 91. Do activity 9.

Hobbies

Fluency

Writing: A Questionnaire

A

Write a free-time questionnaire.

Stage 1: Preparation

Copy the diagram and add to it.

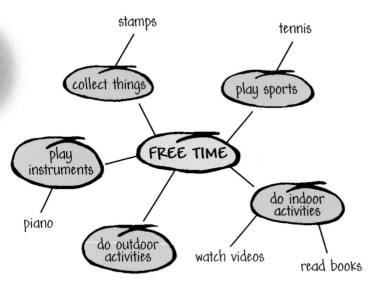

Stage 2: Writing

Choose four activities. Write two questions for each one.

Example: 1 Do you collect things? Yes / No
2 If yes, what do you collect?
....

Stage 3: Checking

Check your questions. Look at the Grammar Reference on page 36

Speaking: A Survey

B

Do your hobbies survey.

Stage 1: Preparation

In pairs, practise your questions.

Example: A: Do you collect things?
B: Yes, I do.
A: What do you collect?

Stage 2: The Survey

Ask other students in your group or class.
Write down the answers in your notebook.

Example: collect things: total 6 (coins 3, stickers 2, stamps 1)

Stage 3: The Results

Put the information on a graph and list the favourites.

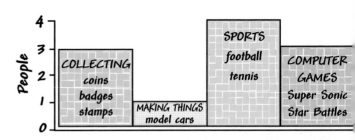

Listening: A Song

C

Listen to the song. Write down five freetime activities you hear.

Consolidation

Grammar

A
BOARD GAME

- You need dice and counters.
- When you land on a square, write the word on a piece of paper.
- Stop when you have ten words.
- Make sentences with your words. You can use the words again for different sentences. You get one point for every sentence.

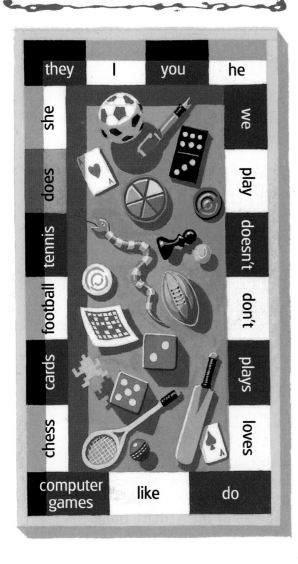

B
Correct the underlined mistakes.

Example: 1 collects

1 My sister <u>collect</u> dolls.
2 What hobbies <u>she like</u>?
3 Does he <u>collects</u> coins?
4 Where <u>he does</u> play football?
5 Ana and Sandra <u>plays</u> computer games.

Vocabulary

C KEYWORDS
Match these verbs with the words in the box: *collect, play, go, read*.

Example: collect dolls

> cycling dolls comics coins tennis the piano
> magazines swimming basketball stamps skiing
> books the guitar dominoes horse riding

Now classify the activities: indoor (I) or outdoor (O).

Pronunciation: Final '*s*'

D

Listen to these words.

Group 1: (/s/) walk*s*   **Group 2:** (/z/) run*s*
Group 3: (/ɪz/) danc*es*

Listen and put these words in group 1, 2 or 3.

plays / collects / makes / watches / gives / looks / chooses / reads

Listen again and repeat the words.

Hobbies

35

Module check

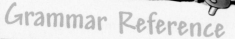

Hobbies (vertical text in left margin)

Grammar Reference

5 Present simple: affirmative and negative

	Affirmative	Negative
I/you/we/they	make	do not make (don't)
he/she/it	makes	does not make (doesn't)

- The **present simple** is used to **express habitual actions**:

George makes model cars. They give her presents.

- We use **don't** and **doesn't** to form the **negative** and we don't add s to the main verb:

He doesn't go sailing in the winter.

We don't watch TV in the evenings.

- **Remember!** Verbs in the **third person singular** end with **s**. The ending of the verb can change a little: he watches / she goes / it flies.

6 Present simple: questions

Questions				
	Do	I/you/we/they	collect	dolls?
	Does	he/she/it		
What When Where How	do	I/you/we/they	read?	
	does	he/she/it		

- For questions, we use the auxiliary do and does.
- You can answer *do/does* questions with *yes* or *no*, or with a *short answer*:

Does he play tennis? Yes. / Yes, he does.

Do you play with dolls? No. / No, I don't.

- You can answer *wh-* questions with *just the information* or a *sentence*.

Where do you play football? In the park. / I play football in the park.

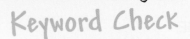

Keyword Check

Verbs: attack, buy, choose, collect, crash, find out, fly, give, help, keep, kill, make, paint, play, read, stop

Hobbies: *collect* badges, coins, dolls, posters, keyrings, stamps, stickers

play board games, cards, chess, computer games, dominoes, football, tennis

go canoeing, cycling, horse riding, swimming

make model aeroplanes, model cars

read books, comics, magazines

play the guitar, the piano, the violin

Times: *on* Sundays, *at* weekends, *in* the evenings, *after* school, *in* the summer, *in* the winter

Places: *at* home, *at* school, *at* my friend's house, *in* the park, *in* the garden, *in* the mountains, *in* the street, *in* the city, *on* the coast

Adjectives: creative, exciting, expensive, interesting, marvellous, original, private, realistic, sinister

---

1 Look at Grammar References 5-6 above and complete Grammar Files 5-6 in the Activity Book. Then do the *Test Yourself: Grammar* on page 25 of the Activity Book.

2 Look at the Keyword Check. Write important new words in your vocabulary book. Then do the *Test Yourself: Vocabulary* on page 25 of the Activity Book.

Lead-in

MODULE OBJECTIVES

IN THIS MODULE YOU WILL ...

Read a questionnaire and some letters.
Listen to a survey, descriptions and a song.
Talk about parties and festivals.
Practise the present simple, personal pronouns and possessive adjectives.
Design a party poster.

a KEYWORDS

In pairs, plan your ideal party. Use the mini-dictionary to help you.

Our ideal party is *(at home/in a restaurant/ in a café/in a garden)* on *(Monday/Tuesday/ Wednesday/Thursday/Friday/Saturday/Sunday)* night from *(6/7/8/9 o'clock)* to *(8/9/10/ 11/12 o'clock)* with our *(friends/family/ schoolmates)*. We have *(crisps/sandwiches/ sweets/soft drinks)*. We wear *(smart/informal)* clothes. We *(play games/dance/sing/talk)*.

b

In pairs, tell the class.

Example: A: Our ideal party is at home on a Saturday night.

B: It starts at eight o'clock and it finishes at ...

10 Party People

Are you a Party Person?

1 Do you like parties?

a) Yes, I love parties.

b) They're OK.

c) No, they're boring. I hate parties.

2 Do you like dancing at parties?

a) Yes, dancing is great fun. I love it.

b) It depends on the music. I don't mind.

c) No, I don't. I sit down all the time.

3 Do you like playing games at parties?

a) Yes, they're good fun.

b) I don't mind playing games.

c) No, I hate party games.

4 Do you like fancy dress parties?

a) Yes, I love them.

b) I don't mind them.

c) No, I don't like them at all.

5 Do you talk a lot at parties?

a) Yes, I talk to a lot of people.

b) I talk to one or two friends.

c) No, I don't talk much.

YOUR SCORE   TOTAL

a) 3 points   0-4: You don't like parties.
b) 2 points   5-9: You like parties.
c) 0 points   10-15: You're a party person!

A

Read the questionnaire. Then listen and write down Mark's answers. Is he a party person?

Example: 1 a

Parties

38

Language Focus: Present Simple - Likes and Dislikes

B

Listen again and complete the sentences with these words.

talking to a lot of people / playing games / wearing silly clothes / dancing / parties

Example: 1 b

1 I love ...
2 I like ... too.
3 I don't mind ...
4 I hate ...
5 I don't like ...

How do you say these sentences in your language?

C

PRONUNCIATION: QUESTIONS
Listen to the questions and repeat them.

D

Use the questionnaire in exercise A to interview your partner. What is his/her score?

E

Complete the dialogue with these words:

don't mind / don't like / love (x2) / do / don't / hate

A: First question. [1] ... you like parties?

B: Yes, of course! I [2] ... them!

A: And what about school lunches?

B: They're okay, I suppose. I [3] ... them.

A: Really? Most people think they're horrible – they [4] ... them. Next question. What do you think of Leonardo DiCaprio?

B: I [5] ... like him much.

A: Oh, most girls [6] ... him. Finally, what about rap music?

B: No, I [7] ... it.

F

Copy the questions from exercise E and add three more.

Examples: Do you like basketball?
Do you like going to the cinema?

G

In pairs, ask and answer your questions.

Example: A: Do you like basketball?
B: I don't mind it.

H LONGMAN DICTIONARY SKILLS

Choose the correct word to complete the sentences. Use the mini-dictionary.

1 His favourite activity is
evening / boring / fishing.

2 Where does he ... his models?
give / keep / help

3 She loves collecting dolls because they are
incredible / horrible / attractive.

(EXTRA TIME)

Look at World Club magazine on page 91.
Do activity 10.

11 Fancy Dress

A KEYWORDS

Match these words with the numbers on the drawings.

> T-shirt long dress skirt jeans trainers shoes
> boots spiky hair shirt mask hat jacket

Example: 1 spiky hair

B

Listen and match these people with the different kinds of fancy dress.

1	punk	a	Paul
2	witch	b	Miriam
3	cowboy	c	Tracy
4	policewoman	d	Patricia
5	vampire	e	Richard

C KEYWORDS

Join the sentences with *but*. Which jobs are the sentences about?

> bus driver air hostess dentist pirate waiter
> soldier gangster jockey nurse clown

Example: I wear a uniform, but I don't wear a hat.

1 I wear a uniform. I don't wear a hat.
2 I work with machines. I don't drive.
3 I work inside. I don't work in an office.
4 I work with people. I don't work with animals.
5 I examine people's mouths. I don't examine their eyes or ears.

E 👤 KEYWORDS

Test Your Vocabulary.

• Write five things you wear on five small pieces of paper in your own language.

• In groups, put all the words face down on the table.

• In turns, take a word and say it in English (1 point).

• The student with the most points wins.

Did you know?

On special occasions, Scottish men wear a skirt called a kilt.

D 🗨️

WHO AM I?

• Choose one of the jobs from exercise C. In pairs, ask your partner five questions.

Examples: Do you wear a uniform? / Do you wear a hat? / Do you work inside? / Do you work with machines? / Do you help people? / Do you work with animals? / Do you like ...?

• You can only answer *yes, no* or *sometimes*. Guess who your partner is.

EXTRA TIME

Look at World Club magazine on page 92. Do activity 11.

41

Parties

YOUR LETTERS

1

We have a special celebration every year on 8th December. It is called Beach Day. We have a big party to celebrate the start of the beach season.
Hugo, Montevideo, Uruguay

2

My grandmother is from Trinidad. Every year in August we go to the Notting Hill Carnival. It is a big street party. We watch the processions – my grandmother's favourite procession is the Masquerade Players. We also dance to reggae music.
Sammy, London, UK

3

Our big celebration is Diwali. For us it is the start of a new year, but it is in October or November. We eat special food. It is also a time to meet your friends and give them presents!
Madhur, New Delhi, India

4

Carnival is usually in February. We elect a Carnival Queen. We dance and carry her through the streets.
Maria, Santa Cruz de Tenerife, Spain

A 🔑 KEYWORDS

When are the main festivals you know?

Example: in July - San Fermín in Spain

in October - Halloween in the USA

January February March April May June July August September October November December

B

Read the letters. When are the festivals?

Example: 1 in December

C

Read the letters again. Answer the questions.

1 Where do they have a big party on 8th December?
2 What procession does Sammy's grandmother like?
3 What music do they have at the Notting Hill Carnival?
4 What do people do in Diwali in India?
5 Who do they carry through the streets in Tenerife?

Language Focus 1: Personal Pronouns and Possessive Adjectives

D

Copy and complete this table:

my / her / them / us / our / his / you

Subject pronoun	Object pronoun	Possessive adjective
I	me	...
you	...	your
he	him	...
she	...	her
it	it	its
we	...	...
they	...	their

E

Complete each sentence.

Example: 1 my

1 In (me/my) town in July (we/us) have a festival.
2 My parents take (I/me/my) to the procession.
3 Do (you/your) have a good festival in (you/your) town?
4 (She/her) always wears (she/her) red dress.
5 (We/Us/Our) parents take (we/us/our) to the dance.

Language Focus 2: Possessive 's

F

How do *you* say these expressions?

> my grandmother's favourite procession
> Sammy's grandmother   my parents' friend

Complete the sentences.

Example: 1 dad's

1 My dad has got a new car. My ... car is new.
2 Fred has got a sister called Jane ... sister is called Jane.
3 My teacher is Mrs Smith. I am in ... class.
4 Alice has got lovely hair. I like it. I like ... hair.
5 My friends have got nice clothes. My ... clothes are nice.

(EXTRA TIME)

Look at World Club magazine on page 92.
Do activity 12.

Fluency

Writing: A Party Poster

A

In pairs, design a poster for a party at your school.

Stage 1: Preparation

Look at the poster above and write notes for your party.

Stage 2: Writing

Use your notes to make a poster on a big sheet of paper.

Stage 3: Checking

Check the spelling of words. Use a dictionary. Display your posters. Choose the best.

Speaking: A Role-play

B

In groups, act out a party situation.

Stage 1: Preparation

Write a name, a place, an age and a job on separate pieces of paper. Use your imagination.

In groups, put the pieces of paper in four sets (names, places, ages, jobs).

Take turns to choose one piece of paper from each set. This is your new identity!

Stage 2: Speaking

Now imagine you are at a party. Ask the other 'party people' questions.
Tell the class about someone.

Example: Nancy is a bus driver from India and she's 87.

Listening: A Song

C

Listen to the song 'Dancing in the Street'. Which of these places do you hear?

London / Chicago / New Orleans / Rome / New York / Barcelona / Brazil / the USSR / L.A. / China

Consolidation

Grammar

A

Put the verb in the correct form.

Example: 1 hates

1 My sister ... (hate) fancy dress parties.
2 She ... (not mind) playing party games.
3 He likes ... (watch) cartoons.
4 We ... (hate) rap music.
5 They love ... (draw).
6 She ... (like) dancing but she ... (not like) playing sport.
7 I can't stand ... (wear) formal clothes.
8 We really love ... (dance) to that music.

B

Complete the letter with these words:

my / I / us / his / her / John's / our / she / Mark's / me / your / their

Example: 1 I

Dear Laura,
My name is Stella. 1 ... am your new penfriend. Here is a photo of 2 ... family. You can see all of 3 ... in it. We are in 4 ... garden. Dad is on the left – 5 ... name is Arthur. And Mum is on the right – 6 ... has got short hair in the photo, but now 7 ... hair is long. You can see 8 ... with my dog, Ben. You can also see my two brothers. 9 ... names are John and Mark. 10 ... hair is dark and 11 ... hair is blond. Please send a photo of 12 ... family.
Best wishes,
Stella

Vocabulary

C   KEYWORDS

Match the verbs and the nouns.

Example: 1 f

1	meet	**a**	a present
2	give	**b**	a party
3	wear	**c**	a bag
4	have	**d**	a person well
5	know	**e**	a uniform
6	carry	**f**	a person at a party

D   KEYWORDS

Here are some clothes with no vowels. What are they?

Example: 1 shoes

1 shs	**2** jns	**3** shrt	**4** trsrs
5 drss	**6** bts	**7** trnrs	**8** jckt

Pronunciation

E

Copy and complete. Match the vowel sounds to the sounds in the names.

teacher / dentist / tennis / reading / red / green / sweets / eggs

	Tess	Steve
Job	dentist	...
Hobby	...	...
Favourite colour	...	green
Favourite food	...	...

Listen to the descriptions and check your answers.

Module check

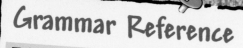

Grammar Reference

7 Likes and dislikes

• To talk about things that **you like**:
He loves dancing. I like playing games.

• To talk about things that **don't interest you very much**:
We don't mind football. Parties are OK.

• To talk about things that **you don't like**:
I don't like dancing. They hate parties.

8 Pronouns and possessive adjectives

Subject pronouns	Object pronoun	Possessive adjective
I	me	my
you	you	your
he	him	his
she	her	her
it	it	its
we	us	our
you	you	your
they	them	their

• **Pronouns** replace **nouns**.
John and Louise love tennis. They play after work.
I play with them.

• **Possessive adjectives** indicate **possession**.
On Fridays, Fred goes to the disco with his friends.
Your books are on the shelf.

• **'s** also indicates **possession**. For singular nouns we use **'s**.
For plural nouns we **only** add the apostrophe.
Mary's dress = The dress belongs to Mary.
('Mary' is singular)
My friends' dog = The dog belongs to my friends.
('My friends' is plural)

Keyword Check

Clothes: boots, dress, fancy dress, hat, jacket, jeans, mask, T-shirt, shirt, shoes, skirt, trainers, uniform

Food and drink: burgers, coke, crisps, hot dogs, sandwiches, sausages, soft drinks, sweets

People: air hostess, astronaut, bus driver, cowboy, dentist, gangster, jockey, nurse, pirate, police officer, punk, schoolmates, soldier, vampire, waiter, witch

Places: café, home, indoors/outdoors, office, restaurant, street

Activities: dancing, drinking, eating, meeting people, playing games, talking

Festivals: carnival, celebration, present, procession

Months: January, February, March, April, May, June, July, August, September, October, November, December

Days: Monday, Tuesday, Wednesday, Thursday, Friday, Saturday, Sunday

Times: 7 o'clock, 8 o'clock

Verbs/nouns: carry a bag, have a party, know a person, meet a person, wear clothes

1 **Look at Grammar References 7-8 above and complete Grammar Files 7-8 in the Activity Book. Then do the *Test Yourself: Grammar* on page 32 of the Activity Book.**

2 **Look at the Keyword Check. Write important new words in your vocabulary book. Then do the *Test Yourself: Vocabulary* on page 32 of the Activity Book.**

Parties

Planet Earth
Lead-in

MODULE OBJECTIVES

IN THIS MODULE YOU WILL ...

Read a tourist brochure.
Listen to a tourist guide, a quiz and a song.
Talk about our planet.
Practise the present continuous tense.
Write a description.

a  KEYWORDS

Match the words in the two boxes.

> the Andes   Asia   the Atlantic   Europe
> the Gobi   the Himalayas   the Mississippi
> the Nile   the Pacific   the Sahara   Spain
> the United States

> continents   countries   oceans
> mountains   rivers   deserts

Can you add more words to the lists?

b

GEOGRAPHY QUIZ

• In pairs, write five questions.

Example:
  Where is the Mississippi?
  What is the capital of the USA?

• Now test another pair.

13 Galactic Tours

A

Look at the aliens. What is funny about them?

> ear eye head mouth
> leg arm finger

Example: They've got one eye.

B

Read and listen to the alien tourist guide's presentation. Complete the text with *is*, *isn't*, *are* or *aren't*.

Example: 1 are

Good morning.
This is the first planet on our tour.
This planet is called Earth. It is not very important, but it is good fun to visit. The people are very strange. They've got two eyes, two legs and two arms!

Please look at the screen. We ¹ ... looking at a city. At the moment it ² ... raining. Many people ³ ... driving cars. And over there is a school bus. The children ⁴ ... going to work, they ⁵ ... going to school.

And there you can see a man in a park. He ⁶ ... going to work. He ⁷ ... walking with a strange animal called a dog. Dogs live in houses with people! Here is a house. The mother and father ⁸ ... eating meat and vegetables. The children ⁹ ... eating. They ¹⁰ ... watching television. And that is a baby. It ¹¹ ... sleeping.

Now, before we begin our visit ...

Planet Earth

Language Focus: Present Continuous

C

Copy and complete the tables.

AFFIRMATIVE		
I	¹am eating (eat)	my dinner.
you / we / they	²... (go)	to school.
he / she / it	³... (sleep)	now.

NEGATIVE		
I	⁴... not eating (eat)	my dinner.
you / we / they	⁵... (go)	to school.
he / she / it	⁶... (sleep)	now.

D

Complete these sentences with the verbs in the present continuous.

Example: I am studying

1 Please be quiet. I ... (study) for the exam.
2 It ... (not rain) now. It's sunny!
3 My parents ... (work) at the moment.
4 Those tourists ... (look) at a monument.
5 She ... (wear) a coat because it's very cold today.
6 The pupils ... (not make) a lot of noise. They ... (work) very hard.
7 Carla ... (do) her English project at the moment.
8 Pete ... (not sleep) – he ... (read) in his bedroom.

E  KEYWORDS

Quickly draw a street scene. Use these ideas.

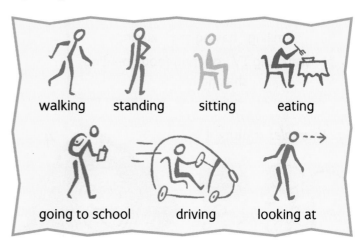

walking   standing   sitting   eating

going to school   driving   looking at

F

Describe your scene to your partner. He/she draws it.

Example: Four children are going to school.

When you finish, compare your pictures.

G  LONGMAN DICTIONARY SKILLS

Look up these words in the mini-dictionary and put them into three groups: nouns, verbs and adjectives.

river   expensive   pull   people
wear   pretty   street   carry   little
eat   marvellous   celebration

(EXTRA TIME)

Look at World Club magazine on page 92.
Do activity 13.

Planet Earth

14 Meeting Humans

A  KEYWORDS

Match the activities with the pictures.

> smiling   having tea   kissing
> watching TV   offering food   reading
> shaking hands

Example: smiling 4

B

In pairs, test your partner about the pictures.

Example: A: She is having tea.
B: Picture 6.
A: Yes, correct.

C

In pairs, read and answer the questionnaire.

Example: A: Number 1 – I kiss them.
B: I don't – I say hello.

Meeting People

1 You are meeting some people for the first time. Do you:
a) kiss them?
b) shake hands?
c) say 'hello'?

2 A person is talking to you. Do you:
a) look at him/her?
b) close your eyes?
c) look at the floor?

3 You are visiting a person's house. Do you:
a) say nice things about his/her house?
b) ask to watch the TV?
c) read a magazine?

4 A person is offering you food, but you don't like it. Do you:
a) say you are not hungry?
b) take some food, but not eat it?
c) say you hate it?

Planet Earth

D

Which things in the questionnaire are rude in your country? Tell the class.

Example: I think it is rude to watch TV when you are visiting a friend.

E

Read the advice for Zorgon visitors. Find three examples of bad advice. Use the mini-dictionary.

G

In pairs, read your advice to your partner. He/she says which is good and bad.

Example:

A: Don't dance the Zorgon Tango when you go to the toilet.

B: Good advice?

A: Yes, it is very dangerous!

Advice for Zorgon visitors to Planet Earth

• Smile and say hello when you meet a human.

• Don't give a human a Zorgon kiss – this is very dangerous.

• Close your eyes when a human is talking to you.

• Say, 'I hate your food – I eat rocks' when a human is offering you food.

• Don't drink petrol in the kitchen – this is also dangerous!

• Sit on the ceiling when you are in a human's house.

Planet Earth

F

Write good and bad advice for aliens visiting your area.

Examples:

Don't eat the ducks when you are in the park. (good advice)

Don't wear clothes when you go out. (bad advice)

Look left and right when you are crossing the road. (good advice)

Did you know?

Every year hundreds of people say they see alien spaceships.

(EXTRA TIME)

Look at World Club magazine on page 92. Do activity 14.

15 The Living Planet

Rainforest

Polar region

Planet Earth

Desert

Language Focus: Present Continuous Questions

C

Listen. Copy and complete the questions.

Example: 1 doing

> 1 What is it ... ?
> 2 Is it ... on the ground?
> 3 Where are you ... ?
> 4 Why is that bird ... ?
> 5 What are they ... ?

D

Put the words in order to make questions.

Example: 1 What are you doing?

1 what / you / are / doing?
2 talking to? / she / who / is
3 they / going? / are / where
4 running? / why / he / is
5 they / swimming / in the river? / are
6 that monkey / eating? / what / is
7 thinking about? / I / am / what
8 those people / why / are / looking at us?

A  KEYWORDS

Match the animals with the habitats in the photos. Use the mini-dictionary.

Example: Camels live in deserts.

> camel gorilla leopard monkey parrot
> penguin polar bear scorpion seal snake

B

Listen to the Zorgon tourists. In what order do they visit the regions in the photos?

E 🔑 KEYWORDS

Look at the picture of the Zorgons in the Antarctic. What is wrong? Write sentences with these words.

> biting   hunting   flying   eating   drinking   sitting

Examples: A scorpion is biting Ziggy.

Zorgons have four arms, not two.

F 💬

MEMORY GAME

- Look at the picture for one minute, then close your book.
- In pairs, ask questions about the picture.
- You get a point if your answer is correct.

Example: A: What is Zed doing?
B: He is taking photos.
A: Correct – one point for you. What is the scorpion doing?

Did you know?

There are about ten million kinds of animals and plants on our planet, but hundreds are disappearing every week!

(EXTRA TIME)

Look at World Club magazine on page 93. Do activity 15.

Fluency

Writing: A Description

A

Write about some aliens on a spaceship.

Stage 1: Preparation

Copy this diagram of a spaceship.

Draw your own aliens in each room. Give them names. What are they doing?

> eat drink sleep look at read study
> play make do write

Stage 2: Writing
Write your description.

Example:

> These aliens are from the planet Bop. They are travelling to the planet Earth. Biff is in room 1. She is looking at a map of the world. Baff and Beff are in room 2. They are playing a strange game called ...

Stage 3: Checking

Check your description. Look at Grammar References 9 and 10 on page 56.

Speaking: Finding Out

B

Stage 1: Preparation

Draw another copy of the spaceship diagram.

Stage 2: Speaking

In pairs, ask and answer questions about your spaceships.

Draw your partner's aliens in the spaceship.

Example: A: Where are your aliens from?
B: The planet Bop.
A: Who is in room 1?
B: Biff. She is the mother.
A: What is she doing?

Listening: A Song

C

Read the questions and use the minidictionary to check vocabulary. Listen to the song and choose the correct answers.

Example: 1 b

1 Ground Control to a) Major John
b) Major Tom.
2 Ten, nine, eight, seven, six, five, four, three, a) two, one, lift-off
b) one, two, lift-off.
3 This is Major Tom to Ground Control, a) I'm walking through the door b) I'm stepping through the door.
4 Planet Earth is
a) green b) blue.
5 I'm feeling very
a) still b)ill.

Consolidation

Grammar

A

Listen to a Zorgon family at home. What are they doing?

Example: 1 They are having lunch.

1 family   2 father   3 daughter
4 son   5 mother

B

What are people you know doing now? Write five sentences.

Example: My grandfather is taking the dog for a walk.

C

Write questions for these answers.

Example: 1 What are you eating?

1 A banana. (What ...)
2 Home. (Where ...)
3 To Anna. (Who ...)
4 A computer magazine. (What ...)
5 A sports programme. (What ...)

D

Choose a picture from *World Club Magazine*. Write a description.

Example: Picture a, page 90

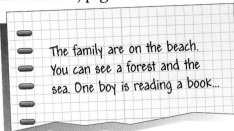

The family are on the beach. You can see a forest and the sea. One boy is reading a book...

E

In groups, read your description. The others find the picture.

Vocabulary

F  KEYWORDS

Match the words below.

Example: 1 e

1	have	a	hello
2	say	b	a jacket
3	turn on	c	a person
4	wear	d	a bag
5	meet	e	tea
6	carry	f	the TV

Pronunciation

G

Listen to these words:

Group 1 (/æ/): *a*nimal   **Group 2** (/ɑː/): d*a*nce

Listen and put these words in the correct group.

Argentina / Arctic / parrot / camel / Africa / banana / kangaroo / arm / planet /fast / Atlantic / Sahara

Module check

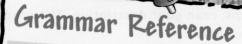

Grammar Reference

9 Present continuous: affirmative and negative

	Affirmative	Negative	
I	am	am not ('m not)	
you/we/they	are	are not (aren't)	looking
he/she/it	is	is not (isn't)	

• We use the **present continuous** to talk about actions **happening now.**

The baby is smiling. The aliens are travelling to Earth. It is not raining. They are not learning English.

10 Present continuous: questions

Questions			
	Am	I	
	Are	you/we/they	going?
	Is	he/she/it	
Where	am	I	
When	are	you/we/they	going?
How	is	he/she/it	

• We use the **present continuous** to ask questions about things **happening now.** You can answer with *yes or no*, or with a *short answer.*

Are the children going to school? Yes. / Yes, they are. Is the Zorgon kissing a human? No. / No, he isn't.

• You can answer *wh-* questions with *just the information* or a *sentence.*

What are the Zorgons drinking? Petrol. / They're drinking petrol.

Keyword Check

Countries: Argentina, Brazil, China, France, Germany, Greece, Italy, Mexico, Portugal, Russia, Spain, the United States, the UK

Geography: The Andes, the Arctic, Asia, the Atlantic, Europe, the Gobi, the Himalayas, the Nile, the Pacific, the Sahara, Spain, the United States

Geographical features: continent, country, desert, mountain, ocean, polar region, rainforest, river

Animals: camel, gorilla, leopard, monkey, parrot, penguin, polar bear, scorpion, seal, snake

Body: arm, ear, eye, finger, leg, mouth

Actions: carry something drive a car, give someone a kiss, have tea, meet a person, run, say hello, shake hands, sit (down), smile, stand, walk

Advice: visit the park, say 'thank you', smile, look left and right, don't ask to watch TV

1 **Look at Grammar References 9-10 above and complete Grammar Files 9-10 in the Activity Book. Then do the *Test Yourself: Grammar* on page 39 of the Activity Book.**

2 **Look at the Keyword Check. Write important new words in your vocabulary book. Then do the *Test Yourself: Vocabulary* on page 39 of the Activity Book.**

Planet Earth

Villages

Lead-in

MODULE OBJECTIVES

IN THIS MODULE YOU WILL ...

Read   about villages and people in Britain.
Listen to dialogues and a quiz about Britain.
Talk   about your area and practise shopping.
Practise there is/are and some/any.
Write   about an imaginary village and play a
            shopping game.

a KEYWORDS

Write a list of places near your home.

Example: a Chinese restaurant, two banks,
an old church

bank bar bus station church cinema disco
health centre hotel park restaurant art gallery
school sports centre supermarket

b

**In pairs, tell your partner about places
you visit.**

Example: A: I go to the supermarket with my
dad. After school, I go to the park
with my friends. And you?

B: I go to the church on Sundays. I
go to the sports centre with my
mum every Friday.

16 Around Britain

Clovelly is a beautiful fishing village in Devon, in the southwest of England. There is a historic harbour with white houses. Near Clovelly there are excellent beaches for swimming and surfing and marvellous countryside. One unusual thing – there is a car park, but there aren't any cars in the village - transport is by foot or by donkey!

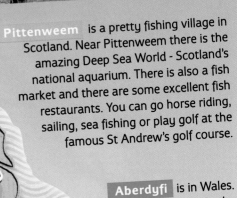

SCOTLAND

ENGLAND

WALES

Pittenweem is a pretty fishing village in Scotland. Near Pittenweem there is the amazing Deep Sea World - Scotland's national aquarium. There is also a fish market and there are some excellent fish restaurants. You can go horse riding, sailing, sea fishing or play golf at the famous St Andrew's golf course.

Aberdyfi is in Wales. There are good shops in the main street and there is an art gallery. There is a great beach and a yacht club. There are fantastic places to visit near Aberdyfi - for example, there are some activity centres, there is pony trekking, there is a beautiful lake and a historic castle.

A ⚷ KEYWORDS

Match the places with the symbols.

art gallery   car park   beach   fish market
castle   golf course   yacht club   harbour

①
②
③
④

⑤
⑥
⑦
⑧

B

Read about the villages. Which village:

1 is in Scotland?
2 has got an art gallery?
3 has got good beaches for surfing?
4 is near a famous golf course?
5 has got white houses?

C

 KEYWORDS

Match these words from the text with the definitions.

> historic unusual beautiful famous marvellous

1 nice to look at
2 important in history
3 very good
4 strange
5 well-known

Language Focus: *There is/are*

D

Copy and complete these sentences about Clovelly with these words:

is / are / isn't / aren't

There	¹...	a historic harbour.
There	²...	a hotel.
There	³...	excellent beaches.
There	⁴...	any cars.

Which verbs are singular and which are plural?

E

Write six sentences about places near your house.

Example: There is a bank. There are four shops. There isn't a cinema.

F

In pairs, find out about places near your partner's house. Answer like this:

Yes, there is. / No, there isn't. / Yes, there are. / No, there aren't.

Example: A: Is there a cinema?
          B: No, there isn't.

G

Write about an ideal village for a holiday. Then tell your partner.

Example:

My ideal village is near the sea. There is a fantastic beach for swimming and surfing. There are places to go at night like cinemas and discos. There is also...

EXTRA TIME

Look at World Club magazine on page 93. Do activity 16.

Villages

17 Village People

Dear Oscar,

Hi! I'm called David. I live in Llanfair PG on the island of Anglesey in Wales. The name in Welsh is Llanfairpwllgwyngyllgogery-chrwyrndrobwllllantysiliogogogoch! You can see why we call it Llanfair PG! There are lots of shops and one hotel in the village. My dad is a mechanic and my mum is a businesswoman. I love music and I play the cello. I am in the school choir too. Every year I sing in the Eisteddfod festival with the school. I'm also learning to surf, because in Anglesey there are great beaches for surfing. Sometimes I go fishing to the river at

Dear Alicia,

I'm your new penfriend. My name is Elaine. I'm from Catterline in Scotland. It's a very small village – there is only one shop and a pub! I go to school in Stonehaven by bus – there isn't a secondary school in my village. There's a harbour, but there aren't any fishing boats now. My mum is a doctor and my dad is a police officer. What do your parents do? I love Highland dancing and I go to classes. In the summer I dance at different Highland games. It's great fun. Tell me about

A

Read the letters. Copy and complete the table.

	Places in village	Parents' jobs	Hobbies	Festivals
Elaine	shop			Highland games
David				

B

Read the letters again and answer these questions. '

Example: 1 Because there isn't a secondary school in her village.

1 Why does Elaine go to school by bus?
2 Why does she go to the Highland games?
3 Why do people call David's village Llanfair PG?
4 Why is David learning to surf?

C    KEYWORDS

Listen to Elaine and David to find four differences in the letters. Use the words below to help you.

Example: Elaine's mum isn't a doctor – she's a dentist.

> lawyer   teacher   waiter
> journalist   businessman/woman
> police officer   dentist   mechanic

D

PRONUNCIATION: CONTRACTIONS

Listen and write the sentences. Then count the words. Contractions are two words.
Example: 1 There isn't a disco in the village. = 8 words

Listen again and repeat.

E

Write five sentences about you and your family or friends. Use the word *because*.

Example: I come to school by bus because I don't live in this town. My sister goes to ballet classes because she loves dancing.

F

In pairs, tell your partner about you, your family and friends.

Example: A: I come to school by bus.
B: Why?
A: Because I don't live in this town.

G   DICTIONARY SKILLS

The words underlined have more than one meaning. Look them up in the mini-dictionary and write the number of the appropriate meaning.

1 Poland is a large <u>country</u>.
2 That <u>poor</u> little bird is trying to fly, but it can't.
3 There is an <u>old</u> castle near the harbour.
4 I don't like <u>tea</u>. I prefer coffee.
5 It's a very <u>thin</u> book. You can read it quickly.

Did you know?

It is very bad to call people from Scotland or Wales 'English'. They are British (or Welsh or Scottish)!

 EXTRA TIME

Look at World Club magazine on page 94. Do activity 17.

18 Village Shops

A 🔑 KEYWORDS

Match the pictures with these words.

> clothes   comics   sweets   cassettes
> computer games   ice cream   crisps
> fizzy drinks   cakes

B 💬

In pairs, find out what things your partner buys.

Example: A: Do you buy computer games?
　　　　　B: Yes, I do.

C 📼

Listen to a girl in a village shop. Answer these questions.

1　Which of the things from exercise A does she buy?
2　How much does she spend?
　 a) £5.40   b) £8.40   c) £9.40

Language Focus: *Some/Any*

D

Look at these sentences.

> **AFFIRMATIVE**
>
> I've got *some* music cassettes.

> **NEGATIVE**
>
> I haven't got *any* computer games

> **QUESTIONS**
>
> Have you got *any* cassettes?

Complete these rules with *some* or *any*.

1 For affirmative sentences we use ...
2 For questions we usually use ...
3 For negative sentences we use ...

E

Complete the sentences with *some* or *any*.

1 She hasn't got ... computer games.
2 He is eating ... sweets.
3 Have they got ... comics?
4 She is making ... cakes.
5 They haven't got ... ice cream.
6 Are there ... fizzy drinks in the fridge?
7 I'd like ... cakes, please.

F

Complete the shop dialogue with *some* or *any*. Then listen and check your answers.

A: Good morning. Can I help you?

B: Yes. Have you got [1] ... comics?

A: No, I'm sorry, we haven't got [2] ... .

B: Well, I'd like [3] ... sweets. Two of those packets, please. And have you got [4] ... fizzy drinks?

A: Yes, we've got [5] ... cola and [6] ... lemonade.

B: A can of cola, please. How much is that?

A: The sweets are two pounds, the drink is 60p that's two pounds sixty, please.

B: Thank you. Bye.

A: Bye.

G

In pairs, practise a shop dialogue like the one in exercise F. Use these prices to help you.

computer game	£35.00
cassette	£8.00
comic	£1.25
ice-cream	85p
sweets	£1.00
can of cola	80p
packet of crisps	40p
T-shirt	£10.00
baseball cap	£3.50

EXTRA TIME

Look at **World Club magazine** on **page 95.**
Do **activity 18.**

Villages

 # Fluency

Writing: Description of a Village

A

In pairs or groups, invent and write about a village.

Stage 1: Preparation

Look at the table. Then copy and complete it with information for your village.

Name:	Bigwig
Location:	Scotland, near the sea
Places:	supermarket, bank, park...
Tourist Attractions:	castle, church
Festivals:	ice-cream festival (August) – ice-cream statues
People:	Mrs Brice (teacher), Mr McDonald (fisherman)

Stage 2: Writing

Write about your village and some of the people. Divide the work between you.

Examples:

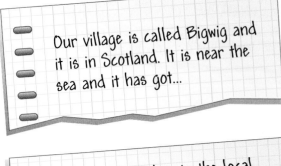

Our village is called Bigwig and it is in Scotland. It is near the sea and it has got...

Julia is a teacher in the local school. She loves...

Stage 3: Checking and presentation

Check your work for punctuation, spelling and grammar.

Make a poster. Draw the village neatly and include your descriptions.

Speaking: Shopping

B

Stage 1: Preparation

Half of the class (village shopkeepers) make a list of six things with a price to sell.

Example: a computer game, £45

The other half of the class (customers) make a list of six objects they want to buy.

Stage 2: Speaking

Form pairs (shopkeeper and customer). Buy and sell objects.

Example: A: Good morning. Can I help you?
B: Hello. Have you got a packet of crisps, please?
A: No, I'm sorry.

You get one point for every object that you buy or sell.

Listening: A Quiz

C

Listen to the quiz and write down the answers to the questions - a, b or c. Then check the answers with your teacher.

Example: 1 c

Consolidation

Grammar

A

Complete the description with these words:

there is, any, there are (x2), there isn't, some

Alastair lives in a village. ¹... three or four shops and ²... a small supermarket, but the village is small and ³... a cinema or a disco. Alastair sometimes goes to town on Saturday with his dad. ⁴... some good shops near the main square. Alastair doesn't buy ⁵... clothes, but he sometimes buys ⁶... cassettes or books.

B

VILLAGE GAME

• Draw two copies of the grid below. On one copy draw five buildings in different squares.

• In pairs, find out where your partner's buildings are. Draw them on the second grid.

• The first one to find all their partner's buildings is the winner!

Example:
A: Is there a building on C2?
B: Yes, there is a house.

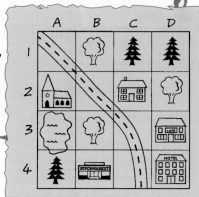

Vocabulary

C

What are these places?

Example: 1 art gallery

1 You can see famous paintings here.
2 You go here to get or change money.
3 You can have lunch or dinner here.
4 You buy food here.
5 You go here if you like music and dancing.
6 You go here if you are ill.
7 You go here to learn and see friends.

D

PERSONAL SPELLING TEST

• Look through the module and write ten words that are difficult for you to spell.
• Learn the spellings at home.
• In the next class, give your spelling list to a partner and test each other.

Pronunciation

E

Listen and repeat the sounds in these words:

Group 1 (/ɪ/): chip **Group 2** (/iː/): cheap

Listen. Which word do you hear?

1 his / he's
2 it / eat
3 live / leave
4 this / these
5 fit / feet

Module check

Grammar Reference

11 There is / there are

- We use **there is / there are** to indicate **what is present:**

There's a very old church in my village.
There are many churches in the city.

- We use **there is not (isn't)** and **there are not (aren't)** to indicate **what is not present:**

There isn't a park and there aren't many hotels

- **There is / there isn't** is for **singular things.**

There is a harbour but there isn't a boat club.

- **There are / there aren't** is for **plural things.**

There aren't any shops but there are two hotels.

12 Some / any

	Affirmative	Negative	Questions
singular	a	a	a
plural + uncountable	some	any	any

- We use **a** for singular nouns.

I have a cat, a dog and a fish.

- We use **some** in affirmative sentences and **any** in negatives and questions.

I'd like some crisps and some lemonade, please.
We haven't got any crisps or any lemonade.
Is there any lemonade? Are there any crisps?

Keyword Check

Buildings: art gallery, bank, bar, beach, castle, church, cinema, disco, golf course, harbour, health centre, hotel, market, park, restaurant, school, shop, supermarket

Adjectives: beautiful, busy, excellent, famous, historic, interesting, marvellous, pretty, unusual

Activities: dancing, fishing, horse riding, sailing, singing, surfing

Jobs: businessman/woman, dentist, doctor, journalist, lawyer, mechanic, police officer, teacher, waiter

Shopping: cakes, can (of cola/lemonade), cassettes, clothes, comics, computer games, crisps, fizzy drinks, ice-cream, packet (of sweets/crisps), sweets

Shopping expressions: Good morning. Can I help you? / I'd like some..., please. / I'm sorry, we haven't got any. / How much is that, please? / That's three pounds, please. / Here you are. / Thank you very much. Goodbye.

1 Look at Grammar References 11-12 above and complete Grammar Files 11-12 in the Activity Book. Then do the *Test Yourself: Grammar* on page 46 of the Activity Book.

2 Look at the Keyword Check. Write important new words in your vocabulary book. Then do the *Test Yourself: Vocabulary* on page 46 of the Activity Book.

Villages

The Wild West

MODULE OBJECTIVES

IN THIS MODULE YOU WILL ...

Read about Native Americans and a literature extract.

Talk about life in the Wild West and your own life.

Listen to a story and two songs.

Write a short biography.

Practise the past simple tense.

Lead-in

a 🔑 KEYWORDS

Which of these things can you see in Wild West films?

chief police officer sheriff bow and arrow
gun log cabin tepee wolf rocket castle
buffalo tiger

b

In pairs, read these sentences. Decide which one is false.

1 Native American people originated in Asia.
2 All North American Indians lived in tepees.
3 Europeans killed all the buffaloes by the 1880s.
4 Many Indians live on reservations in the USA today.
5 The Indians didn't have horses before the Spanish arrived.

19 Native Americans

The Plains Indians

The Plains Indians didn't live in one place. When they travelled, dogs carried and pulled their things. They didn't have horses until the Spanish arrived in America. Some of their horses escaped. The Indians learned to ride the horses and used them when they hunted buffaloes.

The Indians cooked the buffalo meat. They used the skins for clothes. They used the bones for knives, arrows and spears. They lived in tepees (tents made of buffalo skins) and they painted pictures on them.

Indians loved their children. Mothers carried babies on their backs. Children didn't go to school! They learned everything from their parents. They played with dolls and organised fighting competitions. They played in rivers in the summer and in snow in the winter.

Life for the Indians changed when Europeans arrived. Standing Bear, an Indian chief, said "The plains were not wild for us. Then people arrived from the East and the 'Wild West' started."

A KEYWORDS

Match the words in the box with the numbers in the picture.

buffalo   horse   dog   knife   spear   animal skins

B

Read about the Plains Indians. Copy and complete the table.

weapons:	bow and arrow, spear
transport:	
food:	
homes:	
education:	
children's games:	

D

Complete the sentences.

Example: 1 hunted

1 The Indians ... buffaloes.
2 They ... in houses.
3 They ... pictures on the tents.
4 The children ... to school.
5 They ... skins to make clothes.
6 They ... to ride horses.

E

Use the notes to write sentences about the life of an Indian woman.

Example: She lived in a tepee.

> live in a tepee / work at home / cook for family / look after her children / not hunt buffaloes / then Europeans arrive in her area / her life change / live on a reservation / not like her new life

F

TRUE/FALSE GAME

- Write sentences about the Plains Indians. Use these verbs:

  play / travel / cook / hunt / use / live

- In pairs, take turns to say your sentences. Say if they are true or false.

Example: A: They hunted crocodiles.
     B: False!

Language Focus: Past Simple (regular verbs)

C

Copy and complete the table with these verbs:

changed / pulled / didn't live / didn't have / arrived / escaped / learned / cooked / used / painted / carried / played / organised / started

Affirmative		
infinitive + d		change**d**
	+ ed	pull**ed**
infinitive ~~y~~ + ied		carr**ied**

Negative	
did not + infinitive (didn't)	**didn't** live

(EXTRA TIME)

Look at World Club magazine on page 95. Do activity 19.

1 Pat Garrett discovered that Billy was at a friend's house. Pat arrived at the house. Next, he pulled out his gun and killed Billy. Billy died on July 14th 1881.

2 At the age of fifteen, Billy killed a man in a gunfight. After that he joined a gang of gunmen and started to live a life of crime.

3 Billy the Kid was born in 1859 in the east of the United States. Then Billy and his mother travelled west by train.

4 Sheriff Pat Garrett captured Billy and put him in prison. But Billy killed two guards and escaped from the prison.

The Wild West

A KEYWORDS

Find these things in the pictures.

prison guard   gunman   prison
gunfight   sheriff   gun

B

Read the story and put it in the correct order.

C

Listen to the story and check your answers.

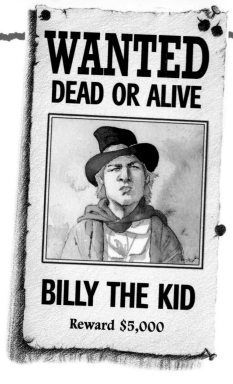

WANTED
DEAD OR ALIVE

BILLY THE KID
Reward $5,000

D

PRONUNCIATION: 'ED' ENDINGS

Listen and repeat these verbs.
1 mov**ed** travell**ed** arriv**ed** us**ed** pull**ed**
2 lik**ed** cook**ed** escap**ed** help**ed**
3 hunt**ed** paint**ed** start**ed**

E

Choose the correct words.

Example: 1 After that

We moved to New Mexico in 1870. (¹*After/*
After that), my mother died. I killed a man
in a gunfight. (²*When/Then*) I escaped from the
town. (³*Next/Before*) I joined a gang. Pat Garret
captured me, (⁴*but/after*) I escaped.

F

**Close your books. In pairs, what can you
remember about the story?**

Example: A: Billy the Kid moved to the west.
    B: Then his mother ...

G

Listen and complete the song about Billy the Kid.

Billy the Kid

This is a song about Billy the Kid,
This is the story of things that he did.
In the Wild West a long time ago
He ¹ ... and he died down in old Mexico.
Billy the Kid, Billy the Kid, poor Billy the Kid!

Pat Garrett, the Sheriff, ² ... Billy the Kid,
But he put him in prison for the things that
he did.
But Billy ³ ... and he ⁴ ... to run,
He said "No one can catch me now,
I'm number one!"
Billy the Kid, Billy the Kid, poor Billy the Kid!

Now on the sad night when poor Billy ⁵ ...
He said to his friends, I'm not satisfied.
Twenty-one men I ⁶ .., that is true,
Now sheriff Pat Garrett is number twenty-two."
Billy the Kid, Billy the Kid, poor Billy the Kid!

Now this is how Billy's life came to an end,
He stayed one night at the house
of a friend,
Pat Garrett ⁷ ... in, saw Billy in bed,
He ⁸ ... out his gun and poor Billy was dead.
Billy the Kid, Billy the Kid, poor Billy the Kid!

EXTRA TIME

Look at World Club magazine on page 95.
Do activity 20.

The Wild West

21 The Little House

3 mlpa
7 lapet
1 rodo
4 robodem
5 krooce
6 bocaprud
2 betal
9 rief
8 gockrin archi

A KEYWORDS

Name the things in the picture.

Example: 1 door

B

Read about the girl and complete this information.

Name: Laura

House:

Number of rooms:

People in family:

Pets:

Likes:

The Little House in the Big Woods

Once upon a time, a girl called Laura lived in a little grey log cabin in the Big Woods of Wisconsin. There weren't other houses or roads and there weren't any people. There were only trees and wild animals. Wolves, bears and wild cats lived in the Big Woods.

The house wasn't very big, but it was a comfortable house. Upstairs there was an attic and downstairs there was a small bedroom and a big room. In the big room there were two windows and two doors, a front door and a back door. There was a cooker, a cupboard with plates in it, and a big table.

One winter evening, when it was cold and there was snow outside, the family were warm and comfortable in their little house. Laura, her father and her sister Mary were in front of the fire. Her mother was in her rocking chair next to baby Carrie. The cat and the dog were asleep in front of the fire. Laura was very happy. She loved her father's stories.

Language Focus: Past Simple *to be*

C

Which examples are singular and which are plural?

AFFIRMATIVE
Mother **was** in her rocking chair.
There **were** two windows.

NEGATIVE
There **wasn't** a TV.
The children **weren't** asleep.

QUESTIONS
Where **were** the children?
Was there a lamp in the room?

D

Use the words to write sentences.

Example: 1 The little house was grey.

1 house / the / little / grey / was
2 there / animals / wild / were / woods / the / in
3 the / house / very / big / wasn't
4 bedroom / was / upstairs / there / a / ?

E

Complete with *was/wasn't* or *were/weren't*.

Yesterday at seven o'clock I ^{1} ... at home. My little sisters and I ^{2} ... in the living room in front of the TV. The dog and the cat ^{3} ... in the garden. My father ^{4} ... in the kitchen but my mother ^{5} ... (not) at home. She ^{6} ... at work. When she returned, she asked, " ^{7} ... your little sisters good?" "No, they ^{8} ...," I said.

F

In pairs, ask your partner questions like this:

Example: A: Where were you at 6 o'clock in the morning yesterday?
B: I was in bed!

1 six o'clock in the morning (6.00 a.m.)
2 half past nine in the morning (9.30 a.m.)
3 two o'clock in the afternoon (2.00 p.m.)
4 a quarter past seven in the evening (7.15 p.m.)
5 a quarter to twelve at night (11.45 p.m.)

G   DICTIONARY SKILLS

Choose the correct word to complete the sentences. Look them up in the mini-dictionary. Do you need a noun, a verb or an adjective?

1 The room was warm and she was ...
sleep / sleepy
2 He wants to be a famous badminton ...
play / player
3 We always have a lot of ... in the holidays.
fun / funny
4 Billy the Kid's ... was very exciting.
life / live

 EXTRA TIME

Look at World Club magazine on page 96. Do activity 21.

The Wild West

Fluency

Writing: A Biography

A

Write a short biography of the life of Annie Oakley,
The Greatest Shot in the West.

Stage 1: Preparation

Read the notes:

- is born in Ohio - family poor - lives log cabin
- father dies - Annie nine years old
- starts shooting animals (rabbits, birds) for family to eat
- enters shooting competition - receives prize
- performs incredible shooting tricks
- is very famous - dies in 1926

Stage 2: Writing

Write your notes in sentences in the past simple. Use *then,*
after that, next, and and *but.*

Example: She was born in Ohio. Her family was poor and
they lived in a log cabin. Then her father died.

Stage 3: Checking

Check your writing for spelling and punctuation.

Speaking: My Life

B

In pairs, tell your partner about your life.

Stage 1: Preparation

Think about your life. Here are some ideas:

~ was born in ...
~ liked/didn't like my first day at school
~ my first teacher was called ...
~ she/he was very ...
~ my best friend was ...
~ started ... when I was ...

Example: I was born in 1990 in
Mar del Plata.

Stage 2: Speaking

Tell your partner about your life. Include one piece of *false* information. At the end, your partner guesses what was false.

Listening: A Song

C

Listen to the song. Complete the chorus.

Oh! Susana! ^{1} ... you cry for ^{2} ... I ^{3} ... from Alabama ^{4} ... my banjo on ^{5} ... knee.

Consolidation

A

Complete the text with the past simple.

Example: 1 robbed

Butch Cassidy ¹ ... *(rob)* banks and trains with the 'Sundance Kid'. People ² ... *(call)* them the Wild Bunch. The sheriffs ³ ... *(want)* to catch them. So Butch and the Sundance Kid ⁴ ... *(decide)* to go to South America. They ⁵ ... *(travel)* to Bolivia, but they ⁶ ... *(not stop)* robbing banks. The Bolivian army ⁷ ... *(follow)* them. Butch ⁸ ... *(return)* to the United States. People think the Sundance Kid ⁹ ... *(not escape)* and the army ¹⁰ ... *(kill)* him.

B
TEAM GAME

- Make sentences using words from your cowboy's gun. You can use a word more than once.
- Take turns to say a sentence.
- The team with the most correct sentences is the winner. The teacher is the referee.

Example: He walked to school.

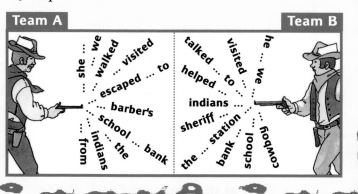

Vocabulary

C KEYWORDS

Write the plural of these words and classify them in these groups.

buffalo knife bear child
baby cook person wolf
gunman spear

Animals	Weapons	Person
buffaloes	knives	children

Pronunciation: Stress

D

Listen to the words. Copy and mark the main stress.

Examples: cárried, escáped

carried / escaped / arrived / travelled / started / recovered / returned / continued / performed / painted

Module check

Grammar Reference

13 Past simple: affirmative and negative (regular verbs)

	Affirmative	Negative
I/you/he/she/it/we/they	hunted	didn't hunt

- The **past simple** describes a finished action in the past:
- Regular affirmative verbs end in **d** or **ed**:

The Indians lived in tepees and they hunted buffaloes.

- We use **didn't** + infinitive to form the negative (don't add **d** or **ed** to the main verb):

The Spanish **didn't hunt** horses in America.

Billy the Kid **didn't die** in a prison.

14 Past simple: *to be*

	Affirmative	Negative
there/I/he/she/it	was	was not (wasn't)
there/you/we/they	were	were not (weren't)

Questions	
Was	there/I/he/she/it?
Were	there/you/we/they?

We use **was** / **were** to:

- Describe a state or a condition in the past:

The Indians were not rich but they were happy.

- Indicate things that were/weren't present:

There was a table. There weren't any chairs outside.

- Express age in the past:

Billy the Kid was 21 years old when he died.

- Say where people were from in the past.

My grandmother was from Kentucky.

Keyword Check

Animals: bear, birds, buffalo, dog, horse, rabbit, wildcat, wolf

People: chief, gang, guard, gunman, sheriff

House: bedroom, cooker, door, downstairs, fire, lamp, log cabin, rocking chair, table, tepee, upstairs, window

Irregular Plurals: babies, buffaloes, children, knives, people, wolves

Weapons: bow and arrow, gun, knife, spear

Verbs: carry, join (a gang), live, hunt, look after, make (clothes), marry, paint, pull out (a gun), ride, rob, shoot, use

Verbs with no object: arrive, be born, die, escape, return, travel

Adjectives: comfortable, dead, famous, wild, incredible, little, poor, sad, satisfied, warm,

Times: six o'clock (6.00), half past six (6.30) a quarter past six (6.15), a quarter to seven (6.45)

Linking words: after that, next, then

1 Look at Grammar References 13-14 above and complete Grammar Files 13-14 in the Activity Book. Then do the *Test Yourself: Grammar* on page 53 of the Activity Book.

2 Look at the Keyword Check. Write important new words in your vocabulary book. Then do the *Test Yourself: Vocabulary* on page 53 of the Activity Book.

Travel
Lead-in

MODULE OBJECTIVES

IN THIS MODULE YOU WILL ...

Read	about explorers and airships.
Listen	to a story.
Talk	about journeys and tell a story.
Practise	using past tense questions and irregular verbs.
Write	an adventure story.

a KEYWORDS

Which of these things are in the pictures?

aeroplane taxi bicycle car train
boat airship motorbike bus

b

In pairs, ask and answer these questions.

Example: A: How do you get to school?
B: By bus. And you?
A: I come on foot.

1 How do you get to school?
2 How do your parents get to work?
3 How do you normally travel on holiday?

22 Gulliver's Travels

A KEYWORDS

Are these adjectives positive (+) or negative (−)?

Examples: tired (−) happy (+)

> tired happy terrible hungry pretty afraid
> fantastic horrible nice friendly

B

A father is telling his daughter a story. Listen and put the pictures in the correct order.

Example: 1 B

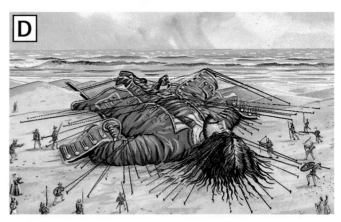

Language Focus: Past Simple Questions

C

Complete the questions.

1 ... he stay on the boat?
2 Where did he ... to?
3 What ... they do?
4 Did they ... him?
5 What ... he have?
6 Where did he ...?
7 When ... Gulliver ... home?

Is the main verb in the past or the infinitive?

D

Put the words in the correct order to make questions.

Example: 1 Did Gulliver sleep for a long time?

1 Gulliver / did / for a long time / sleep?
2 what / did / try to do / Gulliver?
3 how / they / did / attack him?
4 did / talk with the king / Gulliver?
5 more adventures / did / Gulliver / have?

E

Write questions about Gulliver's adventure and match them with the answers.

Example: 1: Why did the boat go down?
      d: There was a storm.

1 why / the boat go down?	a On the beach.
2 where / Gulliver swim to?	b Yes, they did.
3 where / he sleep after the storm?	c Chickens, rice and apples.
4 the little people attack him?	d There was a storm.
5 where / he go with them?	e No, he didn't.
6 what / he have for dinner?	f To an island.
7 who / he talk to?	g The king.
8 Gulliver go home?	h To their city.

F

TEAM GAME

- Play in two teams – team O and team X.
- Take turns to choose a box (e.g. box 2).
- Make a question using the verb.

Example: What did you study in maths yesterday?

- If the question is correct, put O or X in that box.
- You win when you complete a line.
- Choose different verbs and play the game in pairs.

play?	study?	watch?
have?	start?	live?
listen to?	do?	go?

Look at World Club magazine on page 96. Do activity 22.

A KEYWORDS

Match the weather words with the pictures.

warm and sunny icy and snowy
rainy and wet

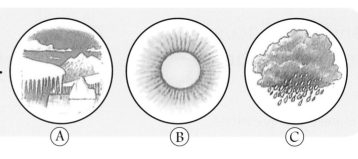

A   B   C

B

Read the text and listen. Match the pictures with the countries.

Example: Picture A – Iceland

The Adventures of Erik and Leif

Erik the Red was born in Norway in 950, but he moved to Iceland when he was a boy. People called him 'the Red' because of his red hair. Life in Iceland was hard and it was a very cold place. Erik had many enemies, and he killed two men. After that, he decided to leave Iceland to escape from his enemies.

In 982, Erik sailed west and discovered a new country. It was cold, icy and snowy, but Erik wanted people to come to this new country, so he called it Greenland. Later, he returned to Greenland with more people in 986. The boats were very small, but they had cows, pigs, sheep and hens with them!

Travel

C

Match the sentences with the years.

Example: Eric was born – 950

1 Eric discovered Greenland.   950
2 Leif was born.   975
3 Leif sailed to America.   982
4 Eric returned to Greenland. 986
5 Eric was born.   1002

D 🎞 PRONUNCIATION: YEARS

Listen to the pronunciation of these years.

1002 = ten-oh-two   1994 = nineteen-ninety-four

Now listen and write the years you hear.

Example: 1 = 1998

Listen again and repeat the years.

E

Look at exercise C. Ask and answer questions with *when*.

Example: A: When was Eric born?

B: He was born in the year 950.

Did you know?

Vikings, like Leif Eriksson, traded with North American Indians 500 years before Columbus 'discovered' America.

EXTRA TIME

Look at World Club magazine on page 97.
Do activity 23.

Leif, Erik's son, was born in 975 and lived with his father in Greenland. Like his father, he wanted to travel. In the summer of 1002, Leif sailed west to look for another country. He discovered a very green and wet place. It had trees and rivers with lots of salmon. This was Canada.

Later, Leif continued his travels south. He discovered another green and beautiful place. It was warm and sunny and there were different fruits, including grapes. This was part of the modern United States. Leif and his men were probably the first Europeans to visit North America.

Travel

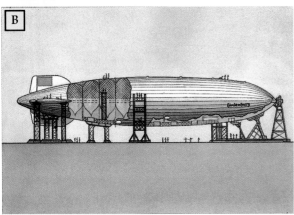

A  KEYWORDS

Find these things in the pictures.

> passengers   lounge   explosion
> cabins   grand piano

B

Read the text and match the paragraphs with the pictures.

Example: 1 B

The Hindenburg

(1) The Zeppelin Company made enormous airships. They were like big ships with dining rooms, lounges and cabins, but they crossed the Atlantic in two days. They were fast; in 1929, an airship called the Graf Zeppelin went round the world in twenty-one days!

(2) On 4th May, 1937, an airship called the Hindenburg began its last flight. It left Germany for the USA. The airship had thirty-five passengers on board.

(3) The passengers on the Hindenburg were very comfortable. They slept in cabins, sat and played cards in a lounge, and ate and drank in a big dining room. In the evenings they listened to music from a grand piano and danced!

(4) On 6th May, the Hindenburg got to the USA, but the passengers did not arrive at their destination. Suddenly, there was an enormous explosion! All the passengers died.

Travel

C

Read the text again and answer these questions.

Example: 1 airships

1 What did the Zeppelin Company make?
2 When did the *Hindenburg* leave Germany?
3 What did the passengers do in the evenings?
4 Where did the passengers sleep?
5 How many passengers died in the explosion?

Language Focus: Past Simple (irregular verbs)

D

Find the past tense of these verbs in the text.

> get make begin go leave have
> sleep sit eat drink

E

Look at the verbs *play* and *leave* in the boxes. Which verb is irregular?

AFFIRMATIVE
They **played** cards.
It **left** on 4th May.

NEGATIVE
They **didn't play** tennis.
They **didn't leave** on 3rd May.

QUESTIONS
Did they **play** cards?
Did it **leave** on 4th May?

F

Complete the text in the past simple. There is a list of irregular verbs on page 111.

Example: 1 left

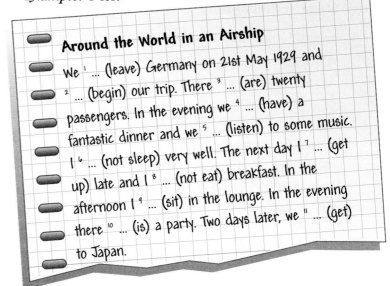

Around the World in an Airship

We ¹ ... (leave) Germany on 21st May 1929 and ² ... (begin) our trip. There ³ ... (are) twenty passengers. In the evening we ⁴ ... (have) a fantastic dinner and we ⁵ ... (listen) to some music. I ⁶ ... (not sleep) very well. The next day I ⁷ ... (get) up) late and I ⁸ ... (not eat) breakfast. In the afternoon I ⁹ ... (sit) in the lounge. In the evening there ¹⁰ ... (is) a party. Two days later, we ¹¹ ... (get) to Japan.

G

In pairs, ask and answer questions about coming to school today.

1 What time did you get up?
2 What did you have for breakfast?
3 How did you travel?
4 Who did you come with?
5 What time did you get to school?

H  DICTIONARY SKILLS

Use the mini-dictionary to find the past simple of these irregular verbs.

catch choose draw fight give hide keep
know say sing speak throw

> EXTRA TIME

Look at World Club magazine on page 97.
Do activity 24.

Travel

Fluency

Writing: A Story

A

Write an adventure story.

Stage 1: Preparation

Invent a character who went to a strange place.
Write notes about the story.

Example:

The trip – Paula goes to visit Aunt in Peru for summer holidays

What happened – plane crashes – Paula alone on island – sees strange animals (describe) – meets people in village – frightened

What happened in the end – Paula builds boat – leaves island

Stage 2: Writing

Use your notes to write the story in the past tense. Include these words: *after that, later, then, next, in the end.*

Example: The plane crashed. Paula got out and saw she was alone. After that she...

Stage 3: Checking

Check your writing for irregular verbs.
Draw a map and illustrate your story.

Speaking: Telling Your Story

B

Tell the group your story.

Stage 1: Preparation

Look at your notes from the writing task.
Practise telling the story to yourself.

Stage 2: Speaking

Tell the other students your story. You can look at your notes, but don't read out your final story.

Listening: Discovery Quiz

C

Try to answer these questions. Then listen to the quiz and check your answers.

1 Where did Columbus first arrive in America?
   a) the Bahamas b) Venezuela

2 Who was the first person to go around the world?
   a) Drake b) Magellan

3 Who was the first European to arrive in Peru?
   a) Cortes b) Pizarro

4 What country did Erik the Red discover in 982?
   a) Iceland b) Greenland

5 Who was the first man to walk on the moon?
   a) Aldrin b) Armstrong

6 Where did the North American Indians originate?
   a) Asia b) Africa

Who won – Sian or James?

Travel

Consolidation

Grammar

A

Complete the text in the past simple.

Last year my parents, sister and I [1] ... (go) on holiday to London and we [2] ... (have) a great time. We [3] ... (stay) in a little hotel near Hyde Park. I [4] ... (sleep) in a room with my big sister. The first morning we [5] ... (have) a big English breakfast. After that, we [6] ... (begin) our trip around London. First, we [7] ... (get) tickets for a tour on an open-top London bus. It [8] ... (be) fantastic and we [9] ... (sit) upstairs. We [10] ... (get off) the bus in Trafalgar Square and [11] ... (have) lunch ~ I [12] ... (eat) a hamburger and [13] ... (drink) a coke. Then we [14] ... (visit) the National Gallery and the British Museum. I was very tired when we [15] ... (leave) the museum. We [16] ... (get) a taxi back to the hotel. That night we [17] ... (go) to bed early!

B

Write questions about the trip in exercise A.

Example: 1 Where did they go?

1 Where / family / go?
2 Where / they / stay?
3 What / they do / after breakfast?
4 How / they travel / around London?
5 What / the girl / have for lunch?
6 What / they do / after lunch?

Now, answer the questions.

C

Write six sentences about your life.

go / begin / make / eat / be born / have / play

Example: I was born in 1988. In 1993 I ...

D

In groups, exchange your sentences from exercise C. Read the sentences and the others guess who it is.

Vocabulary

E

Match the verbs with the transport.

1 ride	a a boat
2 sail	b a bus
3 fly	c a motorbike
4 drive	d a plane
5 catch	e a car

Pronunciation

F

Listen to these words.

Group 1 (/eɪ/): day
Group 2 (/aɪ/): night

Now listen and write the words you hear in the correct group.

Module check

Grammar Reference

15 Past simple: questions

Questions			
	Did	I/you/he/she/it/we/they	stay?
Where When Why	did		

• We use the auxiliary **did** + infinitive and we don't add **d** or **ed** to the main verb:

Did Erik live in Iceland? Where did Gulliver stay?

16 Past simple: irregular verbs

• Verbs that **do not** end in **ed** in the past are **irregular.** (See irregular verb list on page 96.)
• **Affirmative:** use the **irregular** form:

Gulliver swam to an island. He drank a lot of beer.

• **Negative:** use **didn't** + infinitive:

He didn't swim to England. He didn't win the cup.

• **Questions:** use **did** + infinitive:

Did he swim to Lilliput? What did he eat there?

Keyword Check

Transport: airship, bicycle, boat, bus, car, motorbike, plane, train

Travel: cabin, destination, flight, journey, passenger, trip

Places: Canada, Greenland, Germany, Iceland, North America, Norway

Weather: cold, icy, rainy, snowy, warm, wet

Verbs: (present/past): eat/ate, drink/drank, go/went, hurt/hurt, leave/left, meet/met, sail/sailed, sit/sat, sleep/slept, swim/swam

Adjectives: afraid (–), beautiful (+), comfortable (+), enormous (+), friendly (+), happy (+), hard (life) (–), horrible (–), hungry (–), nice (+), pretty (+), tired (–)

Linkers: after that, later, two days later, the next day

Mark your progress in these areas this year. Be honest!

speaking
grammar
reading
writing
pronunciation
vocabulary
listening

key
9–10 = excellent
7–8 = very good
5–6 = good
3–4 = unsatisfactory
1–2 = very poor

1 Look at Grammar References 15–16 above and complete Grammar Files 15–16 in the Activity Book. Then do the *Test Yourself: Grammar* on page 60 of the Activity Book.

2 Look at the Keyword Check. Write important new words in your vocabulary book. Then do the *Test Yourself: Vocabulary* on page 60 of the Activity Book.

Travel

WELCOME TO
WORLD CLUB MAGAZINE!

In this magazine you can: read stories, do puzzles, play games and have fun!
You can also make your own magazine. This symbol  means:
Add this to your magazine! Good luck!!

PLANET DARG

Story Time

Animal Quiz

THE INCAS

Puzzle *time*

1 Puzzle time

Can you find the words in the circles?

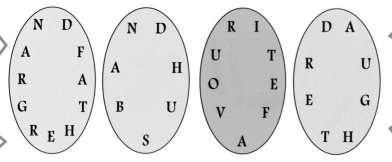

Write three more word circles.
Can your friend find the words?

2 READ THE PICTURES

Look at the picture description. Can you use the pictures to write the description?

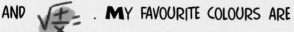

Write your own picture description!

3 Good Parents

Animals are very good parents. Here are some examples.

A female hippo is a good baby-sitter! She looks after the babies of other hippos.

Mother elephants look after baby elephants very carefully. The babies walk under them.

Baby polar bears think cold water is horrible! Their mothers teach them to swim. When they are six months old they are excellent swimmers.

The male penguin has got a difficult job! He sits on the egg for two months. He is cold and hungry. When the baby is born, the mother returns and looks after it.

True or false?

1 Hippos are good babysitters.
2 Elephants are good mothers.
3 Polar bears are good teachers
4 The male penguin is a good father.

Look at the animals on page 106 of the picture dictionary. Choose three or four animals for each of these headings:

These animals are small.
These animals are dangerous.
These animals are big.
These animals are friendly.

 Make a poster with the four groups. Draw the animals.

 4

Animal Quiz

1 Which animal can climb trees?
   a camel / a monkey / a sheep
2 Which animal can swim underwater?
   a dog / a tiger / an alligator
3 Which bird can't fly?
   a parrot / a penguin / a duck
4 Which animal can't jump?
   a snake / a dolphin / a kangaroo
5 Which animal can eat other animals?
   a cow / a rabbit / a lion

 Write your own Quiz! Write three questions.

5 Who is it?

Who is Steve: a, b or c? Read the conversation and find out!

Jane: This is a picture of my brother, Steve.
Sarah: His hair is very short!
Jane: Yes. It's very short and dark.
Sarah: And his nose is very big!

Jane: Steve's nose is big and his eyes are big.
Sarah: Can he play football?
Jane: No, he can't. But he can read. He's very intelligent.

Read about the Swiss Family Robinson.
Can you match the texts to the paragraphs?

THE SWISS FAMILY ROBINSON

1 This story is about a family from Switzerland – the mother, father and their four children – Fritz, Ernest, Jack and little Francis. They are on a ship and suddenly there is a terrible storm. The other people get in a boat and leave the family on the ship!

2 The next morning the storm is finished. The family see an island. They make a boat and go to the island. They take a lot of things and these animals – a cow, some hens, two ducks, two dogs and a very intelligent monkey.

3 They make their new home on the beach. They stay on the island for a long time. They make a tree house and explore. They call the island 'New Switzerland'. They have many adventures. Finally, a ship comes and rescues them.

 Find the odd one out.

1 a) model cars b) model tigers c) model ships

2 a) Japanese b) Holland c) Spain

3 a) basketball b) table tennis c) computer games

4 a) make models b) collect dolls c) study English

5 a) magazines b) stamps c) comics

 Write two more odd-one-outs!

8 WHAT'S THE GAME?

**Look at the picture.
Can you find these games?**

cards   Trivial Pursuit
dominoes   computer game
Game Boy   word puzzle

a
b
c
e
f

9 From you to us!

**Read the e-mail message from a World Club fan.
Now write your e-mail to World Club magazine.**

New Message - 1

Send   Address   Attach   Reply   Reply All   Forward   Draft   Print   Delete   ☒ Log   ☐ Receipt

Normal ▼

My name is Meral. I'm from Turkey. I'm thirteen years old. I've got two brothers- Ahmet and Umut. We've got two goldfish called Skully and Mulder.

My favourite sport is basketball. I play in my school team. In the summer we go to the mountains. I go swimming in the lake.

I like World Club Magazine - it's very interesting. Can we have articles about Leonardo DiCaprio?

Meral

10 Puzzle time

Find out about Carol's likes and dislikes. Follow the strings to the balloons. Then write sentences

She likes ...
She ...
She ...

likes
hates
doesn't mind
dancing
Playing Games
Singing

11

Find the jobs in these anagrams.

1 trawie
2 rai sstohes
3 meafrr
4 nuotsjialr
5 yarwle
6 sneru

 Write three more anagrams. Use page 109 in the Picture Dictionary.

12

Guess the festivals.

❖ You can see fantastic processions. People dance the samba in the streets. It happens in Rio de Janeiro.

❖ It happens on 14th February. People send cards with hearts and flowers to people they love. Usually they don't write their name on the card!

❖ We burn candles and give our friends presents. It is the beginning of a new year in India.

❖ It happens in Britain on November 5th. People have fireworks parties and burn a large doll called a 'guy'.

Answers: 1- Carnival 2- Valentine's Day 3- Diwali 4- Guy Fawkes (Bonfire) Night

 Write about a festival *you* know!

13

Look at the picture. What are the Zorgons doing?

Example: Zizi is drinking.

14

Find the words and write the description.

TheZorgonfamilyarevisitingahuman,Mrs Smith,atherhouse.MrsSmithistalkingtoZed butheiswatchingtelevision.Hiswife,Zeeta,is sittingonthetelevision.Zigislisteningtomusic andeatingrocks.Hissister,Zizi,isdrinking petrolandsleeping.MrsSmithisnotveryhappy.

Write advice for the Zorgons.

Example: Don't sit on the TV.

15 Story Time — PLANET DARG

A. Yin and Yanda escape to the desert of Yarga. They don't have any water and it is very hot. Then hundreds of Dargans attack them. The Dargans take them to their village.

B. Suddenly, a big spaceship arrives. The Dargans disappear and a group of Zorgon tourists come out. The Zorgons are very friendly and they take Yind and Yanda back to planet Alpha.

C. Their spaceship crashes on the planet Darg in the horrible forests. There are enormous trees, snakes and giant insects.

D. A brother and sister called Yind and Yanda live on planet Alpha. One day they decide to explore space in their parent's spaceship.

Read the story carefully. Can you put the paragraphs into the correct order?

16 English or British?

Do you know the difference between English and British? Read and check if you are right. Then write the names of the countries and capitals on the map.

'You speak English. You live in England, in the capital, London. You're English!'

'No, I'm not. I'm studying in London but I'm from Scotland. My family live in Edinburgh, the capital of Scotland. I'm Scottish.'

'OK, you're not English, you're Scottish. So you're not British?'

'I am British! People from England, Scotland, Wales and also Northern Ireland are all British because they live in the British Isles.'

'So people from Cardiff, the capital of Wales, are Welsh and also British?'

'That's right. And people from Belfast, the capital of Northern Ireland, are both Irish and British. It's very simple, you see!'

17 Tiddlehampton

Read Sam's, Daphne's and Captain Darnley-Smith's descriptions. Can you find the houses and cars for each family in the picture? How many jobs can you list?

Example: The Boggis family
house: number 5
Mr Boggis – job: waiter; car: number 1
Mrs Boggis – job: doctor; car: number 8

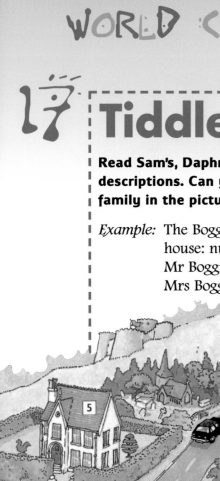

Sam Boggis

Hi!
Welcome to the fantastic village of Tiddlehampton. My mum's the village doctor and my dad's a waiter in the Slugg Arms Hotel. Can you see that big white house with a big garden near the church? That's our house. And we've got two cars! My mum's car is that yellow sports car and my dad's car is white and it's very small.

Captain Darnley-Smith

Good morning. My name's Darnley-Smith, Captain Darnley Smith. I'm a businessman and my wife is a policewoman. Can you see our cars? My car is very big and it's red. My wife's car is new and it's green. And Rupert, my son, loves cars. That old blue car is his car and the big black car is his wife's car. Our family has two houses in the village. We live in one and Rupert and Celia live in the other. The green house with big, red garage doors is our house and the small white house near the river is their house.

Hello. I'm Daphne. Daphne Stott. I'm the teacher at Tiddlehampton School and my husband Eric is a dentist. Can you see my car? That small yellow car is my car. Where do we live? Well, we love colours and our house is blue, with a red door and pink windows. Pink's my favourite colour, you know! And my daughter Lavinia has got a house in the village. That green house, with the blue door and yellow windows, is her house.

Daphne Stott

18 Shopping puzzle

How much money has Sammy got in the end?

Sammy has got £10. He goes to the village shop. He meets his grandmother. She gives him £5 for his birthday. He buys a comic for £1.75 and a cassette for £5.00. Then he goes by bus to the town. The bus costs 50p. He goes to a café and has a lemonade for £1.25 and a hamburger for £3.00. In the street he finds £5.00! He goes to a shop and buys a computer game for £8. Then he walks home.

 Write your own shopping puzzle.

19 Crossword

Do the crossword and find the mystery word.

Mystery word clue: These were very important for the Plains Indians

1 The Plains Indians made spears and arrows out of …
2 They also … with spears.
3 Sometimes the children organised … competitions.
4 The leader was called the … .
5 The women … their babies on their backs.
6 The plains were not … until the Europeans arrived.
7 They used animal skins to make …
8 A tepee is the name of an American Indian …
9 The Europeans put the Indians in …

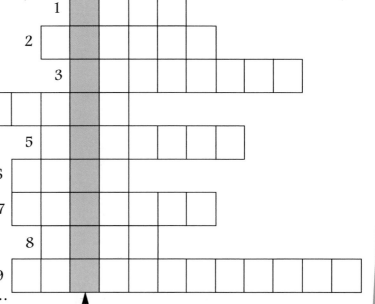

Mystery word

20 True or false Quiz

How much do *you* know about Native Americans and the Inuit? Test your knowledge in this quiz.

1 The Native Americans arrived in America from Siberia.
2 The Sioux Indians lived on the plains.
3 The Sioux Indians were nomadic.
4 The 'Pueblo' Indians lived in Alaska.
5 They constructed houses and villages.
6 The Inuit hunted penguins.
7 The Inuit travelled in kayaks (canoes).
8 The Pacific Coast Indians hunted buffaloes.

Answers: 1- T; 2- T; 3- T; 4- F; 5- T; 6- F; 7- T; 8- F

Scores 1-3: Oh dear, you don't know much!
       4-6: Not bad
       7-8: Amazing! You're an expert!

21

What do you know about the early American civilisations? Read about the Incas.

THE INCAS

500 years ago, there was a great empire in the high Andes mountains of South America. The city of Cuzco was the centre of this Inca Empire. In Cuzco, the great Inca rulers built roads and conquered other peoples around them.

The Inca ruler was called 'Son of the Sun'. He was the leader of the empire and the leader of the army. The soldiers used short wooden clubs for fighting. The Inca noblemen had spears and bright helmets.

Llamas were very important for the Incas. These animals carried loads on the mountain roads and provided wool for clothes and blankets. The Incas did not write, but they counted and kept records using a quipu – a bundle of knotted strings. The Inca Empire ended very suddenly when soldiers from Spain arrived. Today we can still see the ruined city of Machu Picchu, high up in the mountains. And in parts of Peru, we can still hear the language of the Incas.

Match these sentence halves.

Llamas	used spears for fighting.
The quipu	was in Cuzco.
The Inca ruler	were important for their wool.
The Inca noblemen	was a bundle of knotted strings.
The centre of the Inca Empire	was the head of the army

22 History Quiz

Answer these quiz questions.

1 What did Columbus discover?
  a) India b) North America c) America
2 Where did Marco Polo go?
  a) America b) China c) Australia
3 Who sailed around the world first?
  a) Francis Drake b) Magellan c) Pizarro
4 Who was the first person to go to the moon?
  a) David Bowie b) Neil Armstrong
  c) Yuri Gagarin

Answers: 1 - c, 2 - b, 3 - b, 4 - b

 Write your own history quiz.

23

Read about the travels of Charles Darwin and trace his voyage on the map.

Charles Darwin was born in 1809 in a small town in England. When he was young, he decided that he wanted to study botany and geology. In 1831, he joined an expedition to Patagonia in South America. Darwin sailed on the British ship, the Beagle, as a scientist. It was his job to collect and record information about the rocks, plants and animals in South America.

The Beagle sailed across the Atlantic and reached Bahia (now Salvador) in Brazil in spring 1832. Darwin was amazed by the brilliant colours of the flowers and birds he saw. Then they sailed south along the coast. They stopped at places like Montevideo and Buenos Aires. Darwin travelled to the pampas of Argentina and lived among the gauchos. In Patagonia he found fossils of animals which are now extinct.

They sailed to Tierra del Fuego at the southern tip of South America and then north along the coast of Chile. Darwin always wrote his notes and collected rocks, fossils, plants, bird, animals and shells everywhere.

In September 1835, the Beagle reached the Galapagos Islands in the Pacific Ocean, 1000 kilometres west of Ecuador. Darwin was excited to find very different plants and animals on these Islands.

Darwin arrived home in October 1836. During his long voyage he saw many exciting things. He had a lot of questions in his mind. For twenty years he thought and wrote. He finally published his book 'The Origin of Species' in 1859. His ideas of evolution changed our world.

Answer the questions.

1 What was Darwin's job?
2 How long was Darwin's voyage on the Beagle?
3 Which South American countries did Darwin visit?
4 How old was he when he published 'The Origin of Species'?

24 Story Time

THE BOY WHO CRIED WOLF

This story is about a boy from a small village in the mountains. He didn't go to school – he looked after his father's sheep. But the job was very boring.

One day the boy had an idea for a joke to play on the people of the village. He shouted "Wolf! Wolf! Help! A wolf is killing our sheep".

The people of the village ran to the place. The boy laughed and the people saw there was no wolf. They were very angry.

Then, one day, the boy was with the sheep. He saw a big wolf. He shouted "Wolf! Wolf! Help! Come and help me, please." But the people in the village thought, "Oh yes, it's him again. There isn't a wolf". And so they didn't go to help the boy. The wolf killed all the sheep.

Answer these questions:

1 What job did the boy do?
2 What did he shout?
3 Why were the village people angry?
4 Why didn't the people come in the end?

Mini-dictionary

We recommend that you refer to the **Longman New Junior English Dictionary** (published 1993) for words not included here. Remember that this mini-dictionary is not a substitute for a complete dictionary.

A

adventure /əd'ventʃə/ *noun* an exciting story or journey. *adjective* an **adventure** *story;* an **adventure** *holiday.*

afraid /ə'freɪd/ *adjective* feeling fear: *Are you* **afraid** *of the dark?*

after /'ɑːftə/ *preposition* later than; following: *Tomorrow is the day* **after** *today.*

airport /'eəpɔːt/ *noun* a place where planes arrive and leave.

airship
/'eəʃɪp/ *noun*

album /'ælbəm/ *noun* a book with empty pages where you can put stamps, photographs, etc.

alphabet /'ælfəbet/ *noun* the letters of a language in a special order: *The English* **alphabet** *begins with A and ends with Z.*

amphibious /æm'fɪbiəs/ *adjective* of an animal that can live both on land and in water.

arrive /ə'raɪv/ *verb* to get to a place: *They* **arrived** *at the hotel.*

arrow /'ærəʊ/ *noun*
a weapon.

art /ɑːt/ *noun* drawing and painting: *He's very good at* **art**.

art gallery /ɑːt ˌgæləri/ *noun* a building where you can see paintings.

article /'ɑːtɪkəl/ *noun* a piece of writing in a newspaper: *an* **article** *about ships.*

ask /ɑːsk/ *verb* to say something that is a question: *"Who are you?" she* **asked**.

atlas /'ætləs/ *noun* a book of maps, showing countries, rivers, mountains, etc.

attack /ə'tæk/ *verb* to start to fight somebody: *The cowboys* **attacked** *the Indians.*

attractive /ə'træktɪv/ *adjective* pleasing, especially to look at.

axe /æks/ *noun* a weapon.

B

baby /'beɪbi/ *noun* a very young child (or animal).

babysitter /'beɪbiˌsɪtə/ *noun* a person who looks after the children when the parents are not at home.

bad /bæd/ *adjective* not good.

badge /bædʒ/ *noun* something that you wear on your clothes to show your name, your job, the name of your school, etc.

badminton /'bædmɪntən/ *noun* a game like tennis.

bag /bæg/ *noun* something you use for carrying things.

bank /bæŋk/ *noun* a building where you put and keep money.

bar /bɑː/ *noun* a place where you can buy and drink drinks.

baseball /'beɪsbɔːl/ *noun* a sport where you hit a ball and run.

basketball /'bɑːskɪtbɔːl/ *noun* a sport where you throw a ball into a net.

beach /biːtʃ/ *noun* the place next to the sea: *We play football on the* **beach**.

beautiful /'bjuːtɪfəl/ *adjective* good-looking; attractive.

believe /bɪ'liːv/ *verb* to think that somebody is telling the truth: *Don't you* **believe** *me?*

bicycle /'baɪsɪkəl/ *noun*

big /bɪg/ *adjective* of great size, height or weight; large; not small.

bite /baɪt/ (*past:* **bit** /bɪt/) *verb* to cut or wound something with the teeth: *Does your dog* **bite**?

blond /blɒnd/ *adjective* (used of hair) light yellow in colour.

blood /blʌd/ *noun* the red liquid that flows through your body.

board game /'bɔːd geɪm/ *noun* a game like Ludo or Snakes and Ladders.

boat /bəʊt/ *noun*

boring /'bɔːrɪŋ/ *adjective* not interesting: *The film was* **boring** *and I fell asleep.*

born /bɔːn/ *adjective* given life: *She was* **born** *in 1991.*

bow /bəʊ/ *noun* a weapon.

bowl /bəʊl/ *noun* a deep round dish: *Fill the* **bowl** *with water.*

box /bɒks/ *noun* a container with straight sides.

brain /breɪn/ *noun* **1** the part inside your head that you think with. **2** your intelligence.

brilliant /'brɪljənt/ *adjective* very good: *I saw a* **brilliant** *film.*

broomstick /'bruːmˌstɪk, 'brʊm-/ *noun* a long brush used by a witch.

brush /brʌʃ/ *noun*

burn /bɜːn/ *verb* to destroy something with fire: *He **burned** the wood.*

bus /bʌs/ *noun*

bus station /ˈbʌs ˌsteɪʃən/ *noun* the place where buses start and finish.

busy /ˈbɪzi/ *adjective* working; not free; having a lot to do: *He's **busy** now. He's **busy** writing letters.*

buy /baɪ/ (*past:* **bought** /bɔːt/) *verb* to give money for something. *He **buys** a newspaper every day.*

C

cabin /ˈkæbɪn/ *noun* a small house made of wood.

café /ˈkæfeɪ/ *noun* a place where you can buy drinks and simple meals.

can /kæn/ *noun* a metal container with food or drink in it: *A **can** of lemonade.*

canoeing /kəˈnuːɪŋ/ *noun* a sport using a canoe.

cap /kæp/ *noun* a soft hat

car /kɑː/ *noun*

car park /ˈkɑː ˌpɑːk/ *noun* a place where you can leave a car.

card /kɑːd/ *noun* a piece of stiff paper with a picture on the front and a message inside: *a birthday **card**.*

cards /kɑːdz/ *noun* a game

carnival /ˈkɑːnɪvəl/ *noun* a public celebration with processions and dancing.

carry /ˈkæri/ *verb* to hold something and take it somewhere: *I **carry** my bag to school.*

cart /kɑːt/ *noun* a wooden vehicle pulled by horses.

cartoon /kɑːˈtuːn/ *noun* drawings which tell a story: *A Disney **cartoon**.*

cassette /kəˈset/ *noun*

castle /ˈkɑːsəl/ *noun* a large strong building made so that nobody can attack the people inside.

catch /kætʃ/ (*past:* **caught** /kɔːt/) *verb* to run after something and take hold of it.

celebration /ˌseləˈbreɪʃən/ *noun* a special meal or party that you have because something good has happened.

change /tʃeɪndʒ/ *verb* to become or make different: *He **changed** the pictures in his room.*

cheap /tʃiːp/ *adjective* costing little money: *I bought a **cheap** T-shirt.*

chess /tʃes/ *noun* a game played by moving different shaped pieces on a board of black and white squares.

chief /tʃiːf/ *noun* the leader of a tribe of Indians.

child /tʃaɪld/ (plural **children** /ˈtʃɪldrən/) *noun* **1** a young person. **2** a son or daughter.

choose /tʃuːz/ (*past:* **chose** /tʃəʊz/) *verb* to decide from a number of things or people the one you want: *She **chose** to study art.*

church /tʃɜːtʃ/ *noun* a building where Christians meet and pray.

cinema /ˈsɪnəmə/ *noun* a place where you pay to watch a film.

city /ˈsɪti/ *noun* a large town, e.g. London, New York.

climb /klaɪm/ *verb* to go up: *We **climbed** a mountain.*

close /kləʊz/ *verb* to shut: ***Close** the door, please.*

clothes /kləʊðz, kləʊz/ *noun* what you wear, e.g. shirt, jeans, jacket.

cloudy /ˈklaʊdi/ *adjective* (of the sky) grey; not clear blue.

club /klʌb/ *noun* **1** a place where you can go to enjoy yourself, e.g. a yacht club. **2** a long stick used to hit a ball in golf.

coast /kəʊst/ *noun* the land next to the sea: *a town on the **coast**.*

coin /kɔɪn/ *noun* a piece of money made of metal.

cold /kəʊld/ *adjective* not hot: *Snow is very **cold**.*

collect /kəˈlekt/ *verb* to keep lots of things: *He **collects** stamps.*

comfortable /ˈkʌmftəbəl, ˈkʌmfət-/ *adjective* nice, pleasant: *I sat in a **comfortable** chair.*

comic /ˈkɒmɪk/ *noun* something you read with funny stories and pictures.

communicate /kəˈmjuːnɪkeɪt/ *verb* to speak or write to somebody: *If you know English, you can **communicate** with a lot of people.*

computer /kəmˈpjuːtə/ *noun* a machine that stores information.

continent /ˈkɒntɪnənt/ *noun* a large area of land, e.g. Europe, Africa.

cook /kʊk/ *verb* to make food ready to eat by heating it: *He's **cooking** sausages for lunch.*

costume /ˈkɒstjuːm/ *noun* clothes worn for a special reason: *She's wearing a witch's **costume**.*

cottage /ˈkɒtɪdʒ/ *noun* a small attractive house in the country.

count /kaʊnt/ *verb* **1** to say numbers in the right order: *to **count** from 1 to 100.* **2** to find out how many there are: *I **counted** the books - there were 14 of them.*

country /ˈkʌntri/ *noun* **1** a nation with a government, e.g. Argentina, Uruguay. **2** rural areas; not the city.

countryside /ˈkʌntrisaɪd/ *noun* land outside towns and cities.

crash /kræʃ/ *verb* to move into another object with force: *The car **crashed** into the wall.*

creative /kriˈeɪtɪv/ *adjective* having new and original ideas.

crime /kraɪm/ *noun* an action that is wrong and can be punished by the law: *Killing people is a **crime**.*

criminal /ˈkrɪmɪnəl/ *noun* a person who has does something wrong and against the law.

cross /krɒs/ *verb* to travel to the other side of something: *She **crossed** the street.*

cut down /ˌkʌt ˈdaʊn/ *verb* to make something fall to the ground by cutting it: ***cut down** a tree.*

cycle /ˈsaɪkəl/ *verb* to go by bicycle: *She **cycles** to school.*

D

dance /dɑːns/ *verb* to move to music: *We **danced** at the party.*

dangerous /ˈdeɪndʒərəs/ *adjective* something that can hurt you: *Don't play with fire - it's **dangerous**.*

dark /dɑːk/ *adjective* **1** like night; not light or bright: *It was dark, so we hurried home.* **2** of a deep colour: *She has **dark** hair.*

dead /ded/ *adjective* not living: *My grandfather is **dead**.*

decide /dɪˈsaɪd/ *verb* to choose to do something: *We **decided** to have a party.*

desert /ˈdezət/ *noun* a very dry area with not many plants or animals.

Mini-dictionary

destination /ˌdestɪ'neɪʃən/ *noun* the place at the end of your journey.

destruction /dɪ'strʌkʃən/ *noun* the breaking of something completely.

dictionary /'dɪkʃənəri/ *noun* a book that tells you what words mean and how to spell them.

die /daɪ/ *verb* to stop living: *He died in 1956.*

different /'dɪfərənt/ *adjective* not the same: *French and Spanish are different languages.*

difficult /'dɪfɪkəlt/ *adjective* not easy; hard: *This maths problem is difficult.*

disappear /ˌdɪsə'pɪə/ *verb* to go away; be no longer seen: *The boy disappeared round the corner.*

disco /'dɪskəʊ/ *noun* (discotheque) a place where you dance to loud pop music.

discover /dɪ'skʌvə/ *verb* to find or learn about something for the first time: *Did Columbus discover America?*

dive /daɪv/ *verb* to jump into water with you head first.

doll /dɒl/ *noun* a toy made to look like a person, especially a baby, girl or woman.

dominoes /'dɒmɪnəʊz/ *noun* a game played with small flat pieces of wood with spots on.

downstairs /ˌdaʊn'steəz/ *adverb* in or towards the part of the house which is on ground level: *He came downstairs. The kitchen is downstairs.*

draughts /drɑːfts/ *noun* a game played on a board using 24 round pieces.

draw /drɔː/ (*past:* **drew** /druː/) *verb* to make a picture: *He likes drawing pictures.*

drink /drɪŋk/ (*past:* **drank** /dræŋk/) *verb* to take liquid in the mouth: *He drinks tea for breakfast.*

drive /draɪv/ (*past:* **drove** /drəʊv/) *verb* to make a vehicle move in the direction you want: *to drive a car.*

dry /draɪ/ *adjective* not wet; with no water.

E

earring /'ɪərɪŋ/ *noun* a piece of jewellery you wear on your ear.

Earth /ɜːθ/ *noun* the world we live in: *The Earth goes round the sun once a year.*

east /iːst/ *noun* the direction from which the sun comes up in the morning.

eat /iːt/ (*past:* **ate** /et, eɪt/) *verb* to take food in the mouth: *She eats a lot of fruit.*

educational /ˌedjʊ'keɪʃənəl/ *adjective* helping you to learn.

emperor /'empərə/ *noun* a ruler of a big country or several countries.

end /end/ *verb* to finish: *The party ended at 9 o'clock.*

enjoy /ɪn'dʒɔɪ/ *verb* to get pleasure from something: *She enjoys listening to music.*

enormous /ɪ'nɔːməs/ *adjective* very big.

escape /ɪ'skeɪp/ *verb* to run away from a person or place: *He escaped from the police.*

evening /'iːvnɪŋ/ *noun* the time from the end of the afternoon to when you go to bed.

event /ɪ'vent/ *noun* something that happens, often something important or unusual.

excellent /'eksələnt/ *adjective* very good.

excited /ɪk'saɪtɪd/ *adjective* having strong feelings of pleasure; not calm: *I was very excited when I got the letter.*

exciting /ɪk'saɪtɪŋ/ *adjective* causing strong emotions: *I saw an exciting football match.*

expensive /ɪk'spensɪv/ *adjective* costing a lot of money: *A Mercedes is an expensive car.*

expedition /ˌekspə'dɪʃən/ *noun* a journey with a specific purpose, usually scientific or military.

explosion /ɪk'spləʊʒən/ *noun* a sudden loud noise caused, for example, by a bomb.

F

fabulous /'fæbjʊləs/ *adjective* very good; wonderful: *a fabulous holiday.*

factory /'fæktəri/ *noun* a place where people work and make things: *a car factory.*

fair /feə/ *adjective* (of hair) light-coloured; not dark.

family /'fæməli/ *noun* a group of relatives including parents and their children, grandparents, etc.

famous /'feɪməs/ *adjective* well-known: *Prince is a famous singer.*

fancy dress /ˌfænsi 'dres/ *noun* strange clothes that you wear for fun at a party.

fantastic /fæn'tæstɪk/ *adjective* very good.

fashion show /'fæʃən ʃəʊ/ *noun* an event where you can see smart clothes.

fast /fɑːst/ *adjective* quick; not slow.

fat /fæt/ *adjective* having a wide round body: *I think he's too fat.*

favourite /'feɪvərɪt/ *adjective* what you like a lot: *Prince is my favourite singer.*

feather /'feðə/ *noun*

female /'fiːmeɪl/ *adjective* belonging to the sex that has young ones: *The female lion protects her young.*

fight /faɪt/ (*past:* **fought** /fɔːt/) *verb* to use your body or weapons against somebody in a violent way.

figure /'fɪgə/ *noun* a shape, especially the shape of a human body: *I saw a tall figure near the door.*

film /fɪlm/ *noun* what you watch at the cinema.

find out /ˌfaɪnd 'aʊt/ (*past:* **found out** /ˌfaʊnd 'aʊt/) *verb* to discover the facts about something.

fire /faɪə/ *noun* 1 heat and flames that burn and destroy things. 2 burning coal or wood used to make a room warm: *to sit in front of the fire.*

fishing /'fɪʃɪŋ/ *noun* an activity when you try to catch fish.

fizzy /'fɪzi/ *adjective* containing gas: *a fizzy drink.*

flight /flaɪt/ *noun* a journey on a plane.

flower /'flaʊə/ *noun*

fly /flaɪ/ (*past:* **flew** /fluː/) *verb* 1 how a bird travels in the air. 2 to travel in a plane, airship, etc.

follow /'fɒləʊ/ *verb* to go or come after somebody: *He went out and I followed.*

food /fuːd/ *noun* things you eat.

football /'fʊtbɔːl/ *noun* a sport where two teams kick a ball into a goal.

form /fɔːm/ *verb* to make or produce something: *They formed a group.*

friend /frend/ *noun* a person you know and like.

friendly /'frendli/ *adjective* kind and helpful.

fuel /'fjuːəl/ *noun* something that burns to give heat, light or power.

fun /fʌn/ *noun* amusement; a good time: *Parties are fun.*

funfair /'fʌnfeə/ *noun* a place where people go to have fun by riding on special machines.

funny /'fʌni/ *adjective* amusing; something or someone that makes you laugh: *He told a funny story.*

G

game /geɪm/ *noun* something you play for fun: *Let's have a game of chess.*

gang /gæŋ/ *noun* a group of people working together, e.g. criminals.

garden /'gɑːdn/ *noun* a place with grass and flowers.

geography /dʒiˈɒgrəfi, ˈdʒɒgrəfi/ *noun* the study of the countries of the world and things like seas, mountains and weather.

ghost /gəʊst/ *noun* the form of a dead, person that some people believe can be seen.

give /gɪv/ (*past:* **gave** /geɪv/) *verb* to hand or pass something to someone for them to use, or as a present.

glasses /ˈglɑːsɪz/ *noun*

go /gəʊ/ (*past:* **went** /went/) *verb* to move or travel: *I go to school by bus.*

gold /gəʊld/ *noun* a yellow metal that costs a lot of money.

golf /gɒlf/ *noun* a game where you hit a small ball into holes in the ground.

golf course /gɒlf kɔːs/ *noun* the place where you play golf.

good /gʊd/ *adjective* **1** of a high standard: a good school. **2** pleasant: a good party. **3** skilful at something: *She's* good *at languages.*

grand piano /grænd piˈænəʊ/ *noun* a large flat piano.

great /greɪt/ *adjective* very good: *The party was* great.

group /gruːp/ *noun* **1** a number of people or things together: *a group of girls.* **2** a number of people who sing and play popular music together.

guard /gɑːd/ *noun* a person who watches over someone or something to prevent danger or escape.

guess /ges/ *verb* to give an answer that you feel may be right, although you are not sure: *If you don't know the answer,* guess.

guitar /gɪˈtɑː/ *noun*

gun /gʌn/ *noun* a weapon.

gunfight /ˈgʌnfaɪt/ *noun* an act of fighting when guns are used.

gunman /ˈgʌnmən/ *noun* a criminal armed with a gun.

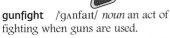

H

happy /ˈhæpi/ *adjective* very pleased: *I am* happy *to see you again.*

harbour /ˈhɑːbə/ *noun* a place on the shore where ships and boats can shelter safely.

hard /hɑːd/ *adjective* **1** not moving or soft when touched: *This ground is too* hard *to dig.* **2** difficult: *a* hard *exam.*

harm /hɑːm/ *verb* to hurt someone or something.

hate /heɪt/ *verb* not to like someone or something at all: *I* hate *snakes.*

have /hæv/ (*past:* **had** /hæd/) *verb* **1** to own; to hold; to keep: *He* has *a good job.* Have *you got a car?* **2** to do something: *We* have *tea for breakfast.*

health centre /ˈhelθ ˌsentə/ *noun* a place where you go to see a doctor or a nurse.

heart /hɑːt/ *noun* **1** the part of your body that pumps blood. **2** your feelings: *He has a kind* heart.

help /help/ *verb* to do something for somebody.

hide /haɪd/ (*past:* **hid** /hɪd/) *verb* to put in a place other people don't know: *Where did you* hide *the money?*

historic /hɪˈstɒrɪk/ *adjective* important in the past.

history /ˈhɪstəri/ *noun* the study of things that happened in the past.

holiday /ˈhɒlɪdi/ *noun* a time when you don't work or go to school: *Next Friday is a* holiday.

home /həʊm/ *noun* the place where you live or are from.

horrible /ˈhɒrɪbəl/ *adjective* not good; not nice.

horse riding /ˈhɔːs ˌraɪdɪŋ/ *noun* the sport of going on a horse.

hospital /ˈhɒspɪtl/ *noun* a building where doctors and nurses care for people who are ill.

hotel /həʊˈtel/ *noun* a place you pay to sleep in: *She stayed at the Ritz* Hotel.

hungry /ˈhʌŋgri/ *adjective* how you feel when you want something to eat.

hunt /hʌnt/ *verb* to look for and kill animals.

hurt /hɜːt/ (*past:* **hurt** /hɜːt/) *verb* to damage part of someone's body and cause pain.

hurt /hɜːt/ *adjective* feeling pain.

I

icy /ˈaɪsi/ *adjective* very cold.

idea /aɪˈdɪə/ *noun* a thought or plan that you form in your mind: *What a good* idea!

ideal /aɪˈdɪəl/ *adjective* the best possible.

identical /aɪˈdentɪkəl/ *adjective* exactly the same.

ill /ɪl/ *adjective* not feeling healthy; unwell.

incredible /ɪnˈkredɪbəl/ *adjective* something you can't believe.

indoors /ˌɪnˈdɔːz/ *adverb* inside a building: *Let's stay* indoors *today.*

informal /ɪnˈfɔːməl/ *adjective* in an easy friendly way and not according to rules.

insect /ˈɪnsekt/ *noun* a very small animal that has six legs: *Bees and ants are* insects.

interesting /ˈɪntrəstɪŋ/ *adjective* something that gets your attention: *I like this book - it's* interesting.

invite /ɪnˈvaɪt/ *verb* to ask somebody to do something nice with you: *I* invited *him to my party.*

island /ˈaɪlənd/ *noun* a piece of land surrounded by water.

J

join /dʒɔɪn/ *verb* to become a member of something: *He* joined *the gang.*

journey /ˈdʒɜːni/ *noun* when you go from one place to another: *I'm going on a* journey *to India.*

jump /dʒʌmp/ *verb* to push yourself up in the air or over something: *He* jumped *over the wall.*

jungle /ˈdʒʌŋgəl/ *noun* a thick forest in hot countries.

K

keep /kiːp/ (*past:* **kept** /kept/) *verb* to store in a particular place: *I* keep *my stamps in an album.*

keyring /ˈkiːrɪŋ/ *noun* a ring on which you keep keys.

kill /kɪl/ *verb* to make a person or animal die.

king /kɪŋ/ *noun* a male ruler of a country: *the* King *of Spain.*

kiss /kɪs/ *verb* to touch someone with your lips, as a sign of love or greeting.

Mini-dictionary

kit /kɪt/ *noun* the things you need for doing a particular sport: *Where's my football* **kit***?*

knife /naɪf/ *noun*

know /nəʊ/ (*past:* **knew** /njuː/) *verb* **1** to have something in your mind which you are sure is true: *I don't* **know** *his name.* **2** to be familiar with a person or place: *Do you* **know** *London?*

L

lake /leɪk/ *noun* a big pool of water with land all round it.

lamp /læmp/ *noun* a small light which you have on a table, etc.

lantern /ˈlæntən/ *noun* a lamp which you can carry.

later /ˈleɪtə/ *adverb* after some time.

leader /ˈliːdə/ *noun* the chief person doing something.

leave /liːv/ (*past:* **left** /left/) *verb* to go away from a place: *The train leaves in five minutes.*

left /left/ *adverb* the opposite direction to right: *Turn left at the corner.*

letter /ˈletə/ *noun* something you write to or receive from another person: *I got a* **letter** *from my penfriend today.*

life /laɪf/ *noun* the time during which someone is alive: *He had a happy* **life.**

light /laɪt/ *noun* something that helps you to see: *He put off the* **light** *and went to sleep.*

like /laɪk/ *verb* to find pleasant; to enjoy: *I* **like** *ice-cream.*

little /ˈlɪtl/ *adjective* small: *The mother was carrying her* **little** *girl.*

live /lɪv/ *verb* **1** to exist: *Kangaroos* **live** *in Australia.* **2** to spend your life: *She* **lives** *in Argentina.*

local /ˈləʊkəl/ *adjective* a place near where you live: *a* **local** *cinema.*

log cabin /ˌlɒg ˈkæbɪn/ *noun* a small house made of wood.

look after /lʊk ˈɑːftə/ *verb* to care for: *I* **looked after** *my baby brother.*

look at /lʊk ət, æt/ *verb* to point your eyes towards something: **Look at** *the blackboard.*

look for /lʊk fə, fɔː/ *verb* to try to find someone or something: *I'm* **looking for** *my key.*

lounge /laʊndʒ/ *noun* a room you can relax in.

ludo /ˈluːdəʊ/ *noun* a board game.

lunch /lʌntʃ/ *noun* a meal you eat in the middle of the day.

M

magazine /ˌmægəˈziːn/ *noun* a book with paper covers, containing stories, articles and pictures, which you buy every week or month.

magic /ˈmædʒɪk/ *noun* clever or strange tricks somebody does to amuse people.

main /meɪn/ *adjective* most important: *the* **main** *street.*

make /meɪk/ (*past:* **made** /meɪd/) *verb* to produce or create: *He* **makes** *model aeroplanes.*

male /meɪl/ *adjective* belonging to the sex which does not give birth to young: *The* **male** *bird is brightly coloured.*

mammal /ˈmæməl/ *noun* an animal that is fed on its mother's milk when young, e.g. a cow.

market /ˈmɑːkɪt/ *noun* a place, often outside, where people come to buy and sell.

marry /ˈmæri/ *verb* to become husband and wife.

married /ˈmærid/ *adjective* having a husband or wife: *a* **married** *man.*

marvellous /ˈmɑːvələs/ *adjective* wonderful; great: *a* **marvellous** *film.*

mask /mɑːsk/ *noun* a covering over all or part of someone's face.

match /mætʃ/ *verb* to be like something else in size, shape, colour, etc: *These shoes don't* **match** *my dress.*

maths /mæθs/ (**mathematics** /ˌmæθəˈmætɪks/) *noun* the study of numbers, shapes, etc.

meet /miːt/ (*past:* **met** /met/) *verb* **1** to see and talk to somebody for the first time: *I* **met** *John at a party.* **2** to see somebody at a fixed time or place: **Meet** *me outside the cinema.*

melt /melt/ *verb* to become a liquid by heating: *The ice is* **melting** *in the sun.*

merchant /ˈmɜːtʃənt/ *noun* a person who buys and sells goods, often buying them in one country and selling them in another.

model /ˈmɒdl/ *noun* a small version of something: *a* **model** *car.*

modern /ˈmɒdən/ *adjective* new, and in the style that is popular now: **modern** *fashion.*

monk /mʌŋk/ *noun* one of a group of men who live together and have given their lives to religion.

monster /ˈmɒnstə/ *noun* a big, frightening animal, usually invented.

motorbike /ˈməʊtəbaɪk/ *noun* a large heavy bicycle worked by an engine.

mountain /ˈmaʊntən/ *noun* a very high hill: *Mount Everest is a* **mountain.**

moustache /məˈstɑːʃ/ *noun* the hair that grows above a man's mouth.

N

nasty /ˈnɑːsti/ *adjective* not nice; bad.

national /ˈnæʃənəl/ *adjective* of or belonging to a country: *a* **national** *doll.*

near /nɪə/ *preposition* not far from; close to: *I live* **near** *the school.*

new /njuː/ *adjective* not old: *I've got a* **new** *bicycle.*

newspaper /ˈnjuːspeɪpə/ *noun* a set of sheets of paper containing news, which is sold every day.

next to /nekst tə, tʊ/ *preposition* beside: *Come and sit* **next to** *me.*

nice /naɪs/ *adjective* good: *This apple is* **nice.**

normal /ˈnɔːməl/ *adjective* usual or expected.

north /nɔːθ/ *noun* the direction that is on the left when you look towards the rising sun: *Manchester is in the* **north** *of England.*

notebook /ˈnəʊtbʊk/ *noun* a book in which you write things that you need to remember.

O

ocean /ˈəʊʃən/ *noun* a very large area of water: *the Atlantic* **Ocean.**

offer /ˈɒfə/ *verb* to show someone that you want to give them something: *I* **offered** *her a chocolate.*

office /ˈɒfɪs/ *noun* a place where people do written work and business.

oil /ɔɪl/ *noun* thick liquid that comes from under the ground or sea, used for making machines run smoothly.

old /əʊld/ *adjective* **1** not new: *I live in an* **old** *house.* **2** not young: *My grandmother is very* **old.** **3** your age: *How* **old** *are you?*

organise /ˈɔːgənaɪz/ *verb* to put things in order: *You must* **organise** *your ideas.*

original /əˈrɪdʒɪnəl, -dʒənəl/ *adjective* new and different: *an* **original** *idea.*

originate /əˈrɪdʒɪneɪt/ *verb* to begin to happen or exist: *This festival* **originated** *in Spain.*

outdoors /aʊtˈdɔːz/ *adverb* outside; in the open air: *It's a nice day; let's play* **outdoors**.

P

packet /ˈpækɪt/ *noun* a small paper or plastic container: *I ate a* **packet** *of crisps.*

paint /peɪnt/ *verb* to put colour on something: *We* **painted** *the room blue.*

pair /peə/ *noun* two things of the same kind that are usually used together: *a* **pair** *of shoes.*

paper /ˈpeɪpə/ *noun* thin material used for writing on: *I haven't got any* **paper**.

parents /ˈpeərənts/ *noun* mother and father.

park /pɑːk/ *noun* a large open space in a town with grass and trees and sometimes a play area for children.

partner /ˈpɑːtnə/ *noun* a person you work or play with.

party /ˈpɑːti/ *noun* a meeting of friends to have fun, dance, play games, etc.

passenger /ˈpæsɪndʒə/ *noun* a person who travels on a bus, train, etc.

pen /pen/ *noun*

pencil /ˈpensəl/ *noun*

penfriend /ˈpenfrend/ *noun* a person from another country you write letters to.

people /ˈpiːpəl/ *noun* the plural of the word person.

person /ˈpɜːsən/ *noun* a man, woman or child.

personal /ˈpɜːsənəl/ *adjective* about a particular person: *a* **personal** *letter.*

pet /pet/ *noun* an animal that lives in your house.

petrol /ˈpetrəl/ *noun* liquid used to work car engines.

piano /piˈænəʊ/ *noun*

picture /ˈpɪktʃə/ *noun* something represented on paper as a drawing, painting or photograph.

picturesque /ˌpɪktʃəˈresk/ *adjective* pretty; like a picture.

piece /piːs/ *noun* one item of something: *a piece of paper.*

plain /pleɪn/ *noun* a large flat piece of country.

plane (aeroplane) /pleɪn/ *noun*

plant /plɑːnt/ *noun* something living that is not an animal: *Trees and vegetables are* **plants**.

play /pleɪ/ *verb* **1** to take part in a game: *I* **play** *football every day.* **2** to use a musical instrument: *I* **play** *the piano.*

player /ˈpleɪə/ *noun* a person who plays a game or a sport: *a tennis* **player**.

poet /ˈpəʊɪt/ *noun* a person who writes poems.

pointed /ˈpɔɪntɪd/ *adjective* having a sharp end.

polar region /ˈpəʊlə ˌriːdʒən/ *noun* the area round the North or South Pole.

pollution /pəˈluːʃən/ *noun* the process of making the air, water or soil dirty and dangerous.

poor /pɔː/ *adjective* **1** not having much money: *She was too* **poor** *to buy new clothes.* **2** needing kindness or help: *Look at that* **poor** *cat. It's hungry.* **3** not of a good standard: *Your writing is* **poor**.

popular /ˈpɒpjʊlə/ *adjective* when lots of people like something: *Football is a* **popular** *sport.*

prefer /prɪˈfɜː/ *verb* to like one thing more than another: *I* **prefer** *swimming to cycling.*

present /ˈprezənt/ *noun* something somebody gives you: *My sister gave me a birthday* **present**.

pretty /ˈprɪti/ *adjective* attractive and nice to look at.

prison /ˈprɪzən/ *noun* a place where criminals are sent as a punishment.

private /ˈpraɪvət/ *adjective* belonging to one person or group; not public: *This garden is* **private**.

procession /prəˈseʃən/ *noun* a line of people or vehicles following one another as part of a ceremony.

pull /pʊl/ *verb* to move something towards you: *He* **pulled** *a book out of his bag.*

pupil /ˈpjuːpəl/ *noun* a person being taught, especially at a school.

puzzle /ˈpʌzəl/ *noun* a game which is difficult to do.

Q

quiet /ˈkwaɪət/ *adjective* having or making very little noise: *He has a* **quiet** *voice, so I can't hear him.*

quiz /kwɪz/ *noun* a competition where you test people by asking questions.

R

race /reɪs/ *noun* a competition to see who can run, swim, walk, etc. fastest.

racket /ˈrækɪt/ *noun* something used to hit the ball in tennis.

railway /ˈreɪlweɪ/ *noun* a track for trains to run on.

read /riːd/ (past: read /red/) *verb* to look at and understand words: *I* **read** *a book yesterday.*

realistic /rɪəˈlɪstɪk/ *adjective* life-like: *The monsters in this game are very* **realistic**.

record /rɪˈkɔːd/ *verb* to write something down so that you can know about it later.

relay /ˈriːleɪ/ *noun* a race where each member of the team runs or swims part of the distance.

repair /rɪˈpeə/ *verb* to make something that is old or broken new again.

restaurant /ˈrestərɒnt/ *noun* a place where you can buy and eat food.

reward /rɪˈwɔːd/ *noun* something given in return for good work, kindness, bravery, etc.

rise /raɪz/ (past: rose /rəʊz/) *verb* to become higher.

river /ˈrɪvə/ *noun* a natural flow of water: *the* **River** *Nile.*

rob /rɒb/ *verb* to take something from a person, a bank or a shop when it is not yours: *They* **robbed** *a bank.*

rock /rɒk/ *noun* a large piece of stone that sticks up out of the ground or sea.

rocket /ˈrɒkɪt/ *noun*

rocking chair /ˈrɒkɪŋ tʃeə/ *noun* a chair that moves gently backwards and forwards.

round /raʊnd/ *adjective* like a ring or circle: *a large* **round** *plate.*

Mini-dictionary

rubber /ˈrʌbə/ *noun*

ruined /ruːɪnd/ *adjective* almost destroyed.

ruler /ˈruːlə/ *noun*

run /rʌn/ (*past:* **ran** /ræn/) *verb* to move very quickly on your feet: *I was late, so I* **ran** *to school.*

S

sad /sæd/ *adjective* not happy.

sail /seɪl/ *verb* to travel by boat or ship.

satisfied /ˈsætɪsfaɪd/ *adjective* pleased; contented.

say /seɪ/ (*past:* **said** /sed/) *verb* to speak something: *He* **said** *hello.*

school /skuːl/ *noun* a place where you study.

schoolmate /ˈskuːlmeɪt/ *noun* a person who is at school with you.

science /ˈsaɪəns/ *noun* the study of nature and how things in the world are made and behave.

screen /skriːn/ *noun* a flat square surface that shows pictures etc. at a cinema, on TV or on a computer.

season /ˈsiːzən/ *noun* one of the four parts of the year, e.g. summer.

sell /sel/ (*past:* **sold** /səʊld/) *verb* to change something for money: *They* **sell** *sweets in the shop.*

sentence /ˈsentəns/ *noun* a group of words making a statement or a question. It begins with a capital letter and ends with a full stop.

serve /sɜːv/ *verb* to help a customer in a shop, restaurant, etc.

shake /ʃeɪk/ (*past:* **shook** /ʃʊk/) *verb* to move quickly from side to side or up and down: *I said hello and we* **shook** *hands.*

sheet /ʃiːt/ *noun* a large thin piece of cloth, usually white, for putting on a bed.

shoot /ʃuːt/ (*past:* **shot** /ʃɒt/) *verb* to use a gun.

shop /ʃɒp/ *noun* a place where you can buy things: *a clothes* **shop.**

short /ʃɔːt/ *adjective* not tall; not long.

silly /ˈsɪli/ *adjective* not serious or sensible.

similar /ˈsɪmɪlə/ *adjective* alike: *Our T-shirts are* **similar.**

sing /sɪŋ/ (*past:* **sang** /sæŋ/) *verb* to make music with your voice.

sinister /ˈsɪnɪstə/ *adjective* something that looks frightening and dangerous.

sit /sɪt/ (*past:* **sat** /sæt/) *verb* to rest on the bottom of your back: *He* **sat** *on a chair.*

ski /skiː/ *verb* to travel on snow wearing long narrow pieces of wood on your feet.

skin /skɪn/ *noun* the outside of your body or an animal's body: *They used animal* **skins** *for clothes.*

sleep /sliːp/ (*past:* **slept** /slept/) *verb* to rest with your eyes closed: *I usually* **sleep** *for nine hours a night.*

sleepy /ˈsliːpi/ *adjective* wanting to sleep: *I felt* **sleepy,** *so I went to bed.*

slowly /ˈsləʊli/ *adverb* to do something in a slow manner: *He walks very* **slowly.**

small /smɔːl/ *adjective* not big.

smart /smɑːt/ *adjective* dressed in good, clean clothes: *She always wears* **smart** *clothes.*

smile /smaɪl/ *verb* to move your mouth to show you are happy.

snow /snəʊ/ *noun* very cold rain which is soft and white.

snowy /ˈsnəʊi/ *adjective* what the weather is like when it snows.

sociable /ˈsəʊʃəbəl/ *adjective* friendly.

soft drink /ˈsɒft drɪŋk/ *noun* a drink with no alcohol in it.

song /sɒŋ/ *noun* a piece of music with words that are sung.

soon /suːn/ *adverb* in a short time: *Come and see me* **soon.**

south /saʊθ/ *noun* the direction that is on the right when you look at the sun at the start of the morning.

speak /spiːk/ (*past:* **spoke** /spəʊk/) *verb* **1** to say words aloud: *Children learn to* **speak** *when they are very small.* **2** to be able to talk in a particular language: *She* **speaks** *Italian.*

spear /spɪə/ *noun* a weapon.

spell /spel/ *verb* to say the letters that make up a word: *You* **spell** *dog, D-O-G.*

spiky /ˈspaɪki/ *adjective* long and pointed: *He's got* **spiky** *hair.*

sports centre /ˈspɔːts ˌsentə/ *noun* a place where you can do different sports for pleasure.

sport /spɔːt/ *noun* games in general: *Football is a* **sport.**

sporty /ˈspɔːti/ *adjective* of a person who loves sports.

spring /sprɪŋ/ *noun* the season between winter and summer.

square /skweə/ *adjective* having four straight sides of equal length: *The window was* **square.**

stamp /stæmp/ *noun*

stand /stænd/ (*past:* **stood** /stʊd/) *verb* to be on your feet.

stick /stɪk/ (*past:* **stuck** /stʌk/) *verb* to fix something with glue: *I* **stuck** *a stamp on the letter.*

sticker /ˈstɪkə/ *noun* something you can stick somewhere.

stop /stɒp/ *verb* to finish doing something: *We* **stopped** *eating.*

storm /stɔːm/ *noun* a time of high winds and sometimes thunder and rain.

strange /streɪndʒ/ *adjective* unusual; not what you are accustomed to.

street /striːt/ *noun* a road with buildings at the side of it.

subject /ˈsʌbdʒɪkt/ *noun* something that you study: *English is one of our school subjects.*

suffer /ˈsʌfə/ *verb* to be in pain or trouble.

summer /ˈsʌmə/ *noun* the season between spring and autumn: *The weather is usually hot in* **summer.**

sunny /ˈsʌni/ *adjective* what the weather is like when it's hot and there are no clouds.

supermarket /ˈsuːpəmɑːkɪt, ˈsjuː-/ *noun* a large shop where you can buy different types of food and drink and things for the house.

surfing /ˈsɜːfɪŋ/ *noun* a sport where you ride on the waves of the sea.

surprised /sə'praɪzd/ *adjective* what you feel when something unexpected happens: *I was* **surprised** *by the news.*

survive /sə'vaɪv/ *verb* to continue to live.

swim /swɪm/ (*past:* **swam** /swæm/) *verb* to move in water.

sword /sɔːd/ *noun* a weapon.

T

take turns to /ˌteɪk 'tɜːnz tə, tʊ/ *verb* to do something one after another.

talk /tɔːk/ *verb* to speak: *I* **talk** *to my friends.*

tall /tɔːl/ *adjective* not short.

taxi /'tæksi/ *noun* a car which takes you on a journey which you pay for.

tea /tiː/ *noun* **1** a hot drink: *We drink* **tea** *for breakfast.* **2** a meal in the afternoon or evening: *We have* **tea** *at six o'clock.*

team /tiːm/ *noun* a group of two or more people who play a game.

tennis /'tenɪs/ *noun* a sport where two or four people hit a ball over a net.

tepee /'tiːpiː/ *noun* an American Indian tent.

terrible /'terɪbəl/ *adjective* very bad.

thin /θɪn/ *adjective* **1** not fat: *He's* **thin** *because he doesn't eat much.* **2** not thick: *This paper is too* **thin.**

think /θɪŋk/ *verb* **1** to use your mind: **Think** *before you speak.* **1** to have an opinion: *What do you* **think** *of my singing?*

throw /θrəʊ/ (*past:* **threw** /θruː/) *verb* to send something through the air with your arms.

ticket /'tɪkɪt/ *noun* a small piece of paper which shows you have paid to travel on a bus, see a film at the cinema, etc.

tired /'taɪəd/ *adjective* needing rest or sleep: *I felt* **tired** *after school.*

town /taʊn/ *noun* a place with many houses and other buildings where people live and work.

toy /tɔɪ/ *noun* something a child plays with.

train /treɪn/ *noun*

travel /'trævəl/ *verb* to go from one place to another.

trick /trɪk/ *noun* an amusing action done to make someone look silly: *Let's play a* **trick** *on him.*

treat /triːt/ *noun* something special which gives you pleasure: *Her birthday* **treat** *was a trip to London.*

trip /trɪp/ *noun* a short journey, usually for pleasure: *a* **trip** *to London.*

try /traɪ/ *verb* to attempt to do something: *He* **tried** *to climb the tree but it was too difficult.*

twin /twɪn/ *noun* one of two children born to the same mother at the same time.

typical /'tɪpɪkəl/ *adjective* the same as other people or things belonging to that group or kind.

U

understand /ˌʌndə'stænd/ (*past:* **understood** /ˌʌndə'stʊd/) *verb* to hear or read something and know what it means.

underwater /ˌʌndə'wɔːtə/ *adverb* below the surface of the water: *He swam* **underwater.**

unhappy /ʌn'hæpi/ *adjective* not happy.

unusual /ʌn'juːʒuəl, -ʒəl/ *adjective* not usual; strange.

upstairs /ˌʌp'steəz/ *adverb* on an upper floor in a building: *She went* **upstairs.**

use /juːz/ *verb* to employ something to do something else: *She* **used** *her new pen to write a story.*

useless /'juːsləs/ *adjective* having no good purpose; not helpful.

V

vegetable /'vedʒtəbəl/ *noun* a plant that you can eat: *Carrots and cabbages are* **vegetables.**

village /'vɪlɪdʒ/ *noun* a small town; a group of houses.

violin /'vaɪələnt/ *noun* a musical instrument.

violent /ˌvaɪə'lɪn/ *adjective* aggressive; using force to hurt someone.

volleyball /'vɒlibɔːl/ *noun* a sport where you knock a large ball backwards and forwards across a net.

voyage /'vɔɪ-ɪdʒ/ *noun* a long journey by sea.

W

walk /wɔːk/ *verb* to move on your feet: *I* **walk** *to school every day.*

walkman /'wɔːkmən/ *noun* a small machine for playing music, which you can carry with you.

wall /wɔːl/ *noun* one of the sides of a building or a room.

war /wɔː/ *noun* a time of fighting between countries.

warm /wɔːm/ *adjective* a temperature between cold and hot.

watch /wɒtʃ/ *noun* a small clock that you wear on your arm.

watch /wɒtʃ/ *verb* to look at (usually with interest).

wear /weə/ (*past:* **wore** /wɔː/) *verb* to have clothes on.

weekend /ˌwiːk'end/ *noun* the time from Friday evening to Sunday evening.

welcome /'welkəm/ *verb* to meet and greet someone with pleasure.

west /west/ *noun* the direction in which the sun goes down.

wet /wet/ *adjective* **1** covered with or containing liquid: *My hair is* **wet.** **2** rainy: *a* **wet** *day.*

whirlpool /'wɜːlpuːl/ *noun* a place in a river or the sea where the water goes round and round.

wild /waɪld/ *adjective* not friendly or domesticated: *Lions are* **wild** *cats.*

Wild West /ˌwaɪld 'west/ *noun* the parts of the United States before people built towns.

winter /'wɪntə/ *noun* the season between autumn and spring: *The weather is usually cold in* **winter.**

wood /wʊd/ *noun* material from trees: *The cabin was made of* **wood.**

wool /wʊl/ *noun* the soft thick hair of sheep.

word /wɜːd/ *noun* a group of letters which mean something: *What's the Spanish* **word** *for 'mouse'?*

work /wɜːk/ *noun* a person's job: *to go to* **work.**

world /wɜːld/ *noun* everything on our planet: *There are a lot of countries in the* **world.**

write /raɪt/ (*past:* **wrote** /rəʊt/) *verb* to communicate using a pen and paper.

wrong /rɒŋ/ *adjective* not correct; not right: *This answer is* **wrong.**

Y

yacht /jɒt/ *noun* a boat with sails

young /jʌŋ/ *adjective* not old; of not many years: *She's three years old - she's very* **young.**

Picture dictionary

Food and drink

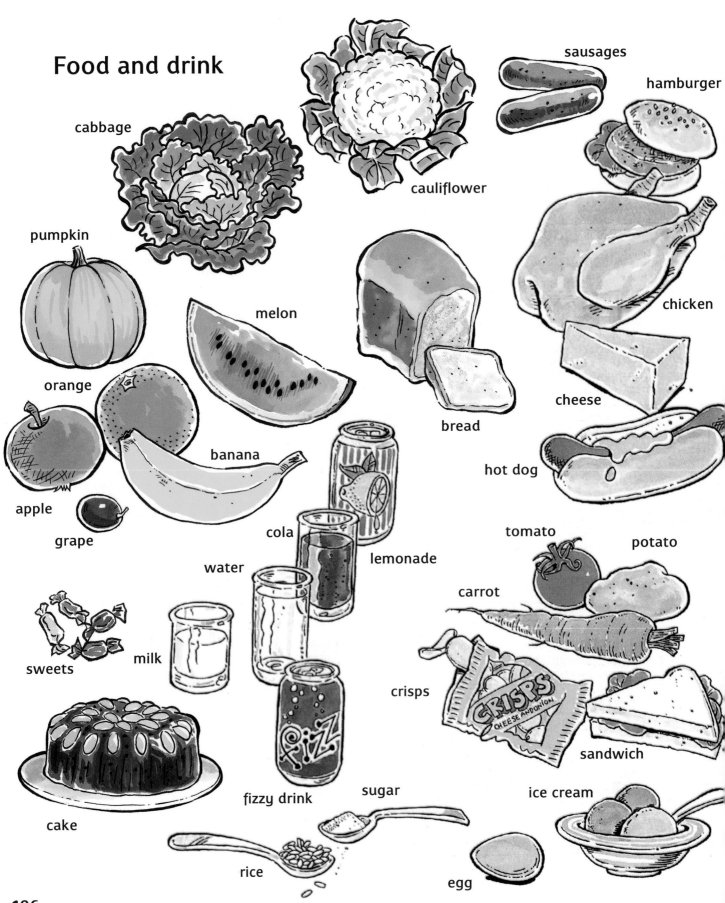

sausages

hamburger

cabbage

cauliflower

pumpkin

melon

chicken

orange

bread

cheese

apple

banana

hot dog

grape

cola

tomato

potato

water

lemonade

carrot

sweets

milk

crisps

sandwich

cake

fizzy drink

sugar

ice cream

rice

egg

House

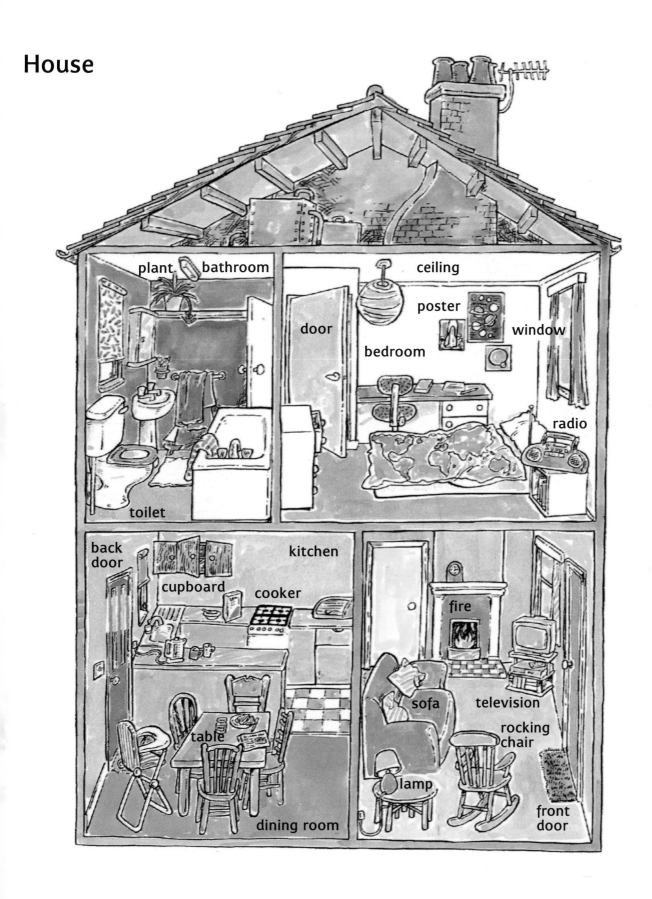

plant · bathroom · ceiling · poster · window · door · bedroom · radio · toilet · back door · kitchen · cupboard · cooker · fire · sofa · television · rocking chair · table · lamp · dining room · front door

Picture dictionary

Families

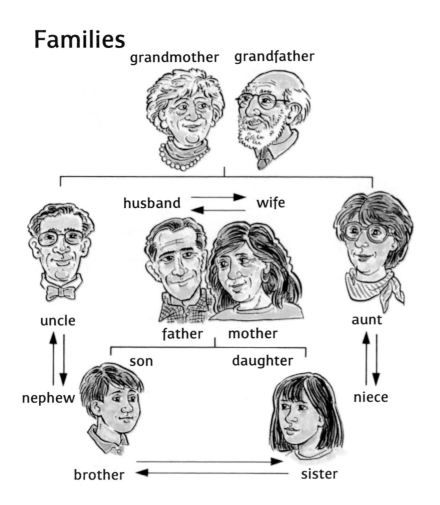

Colours

 blue

 green

 pink

 red

 orange

 yellow

 purple

 brown

 white

 black

 grey

Numbers

Number	Order	Number	Order
1 one	first	13 thirteen	thirteenth
2 two	second	14 fourteen	fourteenth
3 three	third	20 twenty	twentieth
4 four	fourth	21 twenty-one	twenty-first
5 five	fifth	30 thirty	thirtieth
6 six	sixth	40 forty	fortieth
7 seven	seventh	50 fifty	fiftieth
8 eight	eighth	60 sixty	sixtieth
9 nine	ninth	70 seventy	seventieth
10 ten	tenth	80 eighty	eightieth
11 eleven	eleventh	90 ninety	ninetieth
12 twelve	twelfth	100 a hundred	hundredth
		1000 a thousand	thousandth

People

tist

bus driver

farmer

jockey

gardener

writer

air hostess

lawyer

journalist

police officer

mechanic

teacher

cook

nurse

pilot

waiter

astronaut

vampire

secretary

doctor

soldier

businessman

ineer

designer

cowboy

sheriff

businesswoman

Picture dictionary

Animals

whale

bear

rabb

tarantula

buffalo

goldfish

piranha

polar bear

duck

zebra

cat

leopard

scorpion

dog

camel

seal

crocodile

wolf

sheep

horse

lion

tiger

dolphi

cow

panther

gorilla

kangaroo

spider

elephant

jaguar

hippo

pen

fox

snake

monkey

alligator

Irregular verb list

Infinitive	Past tense
begin	began
build	built
buy	bought
come	came
drink	drank
drive	drove
do	did
eat	ate
find	found
fly	flew
get	got
go	went
have	had
hurt	hurt
leave	left
make	made
meet	met
put	put
read	read
ride	rode
run	ran
see	saw
sell	sold
sit	sat
sleep	slept
stand	stood
swim	swam
take	took
understand	understood
wear	wore
write	wrote

End-of-year self-assessment

Assess yourself:

A I have no problems.
B I have some problems.
C I have a lot of problems with this.

Speaking *Writing*

- ☐ ☐ Talking about you, your hobbies, your family, etc.
- ☐ ☐ Using English in the class.
- ☐ ☐ Describing people and places.
- ☐ ☐ Talking about likes and dislikes.
- ☐ ☐ Talking about the past.

Listening

- ☐ to your teacher
- ☐ to dialogues (on the cassette)
- ☐ to other students

Grammar

- ☐ *To be*
- ☐ *Can*
- ☐ *Have got*
- ☐ Present simple
- ☐ Present continuous
- ☐ Past tense
- ☐ Questions
- ☐ *Some /any*

Pearson Education Limited,
Edinburgh Gate
Harlow
Essex CM20 2JE
England
and Associated Companies throughout the World.

www.longman.com

First published 2000
Eighth impression 2004

Set in 12pt Footlight Light and Eurocrat

Printed in Spain by Graficas Estella

ISBN 0582 34973 7

Illustrated by Amy, Bernabeu, Enrique Bernabeu, Fernando Cano, Victor Diaz, Robin Edmonds, Fernando Gómez, Phil Healey, Alberto de Hoyos, Adriana Juárez, Chris Pavely and Chris Simpson.

Acknowledgements

The authors and publishers would like to thank Val Emslie for writing additional materials for World Club 1.

We are also very grateful to the following people and institutions for their contribution:
Mónica Marinakis and her team from AACI;
Marta Moure and Liliana Luna from Asoc.
Ex-Alumnas del Prof. en Lenguas Vivas J.R.F;
Nora Gervasio, Patricia Ugo, Gabriela Atrio y alumnos del Colegio Monseñor Dillon.

We are grateful to the following for permission to reproduce copyright material:
Pearson Education for the adapted song 'Billy the Kid' from Pathway 4 Teacher's Guide by Nicolas Hawke and Donald Dallas © Longman Group UK Ltd (1985).

Photo Acknowledgements

We are grateful to the following for permission to reproduce copyright photographs:
AGE for pages:12 (bottom left), 60 (right) & 77 (bottom). Britain on view for pages: 4 (a), 58 & 60 (left). Chus del Águila for page 8 (right). Columbia for page 67 (bottom). G. Boden for pages: 5 (top right) & 91. Image Bank for pages: 4(h), 28 (right), & 32 (right). Incolor for pages: 6, 8 (background), 12 (top left & right), 13, 32 (left), 47 (background), 57 & 77 (middle). Javier Jaime for page 5. Longman Photographic Unit for pages: 4 (g), 27, 28 (left) & 62. Ronald Grant Archive for page 67 (top). Stock Market for page 77 (top). Superstock for page 42 (top). Telegraph Colour Library for page 52 (top left). Tony Stone for pages: 10, 52 (bottom left) & 52 (right). Zardoya for pages: 4 (c, b), 7 (left), 8 (left), 27 (bottom right), 37 & 77 (middle middle).